The Complete Dr. Nowzaradan Diet

1200-Calorie Approach with a 1000-Day Tracking Journal, Low-Cost Recipes, and Expert Strategies. 30-Day Meal Plan Included!

Demetris Becker

© Copyright 2024 - All rights reserved.

The contents of this book may not be reproduced or transmitted without written permission from the author or publisher. Under no circumstances can the publisher or author be held liable or liable for any damages, compensation, or loss of money arising from this book's information, whether directly or indirectly.

About The Author

Demetris Becker was born in North California in 1989. He is a chef and nutritionist from the USA. He graduated in Nutrition and Food Science at the University of North Texas. Then he worked under a health specialist for 5 years. This book is part of his passion of writing and personal experiences.

Table OF Contents

INTRODUCTION 12
PART 1: Fundamental Knowledge 13
What You Need to Know About Diet 13
About The Diet 13
The Benefits 14
Dr. Nowzaradan's Keto Symphony Diet Plan 16
Recommended Food List 17
Foods to Avoid 19
PART 2: The Recipes 20
BREAKFAST 20
1. Chia Seed Pudding 20
2. Avocado and Bacon Egg Cups 20
3. Omelet 21
4. Chicken with Green Beans 22
5. Broccoli and Pasta 22
6. Waffle Sandwich 23
7. Berry Chia Pudding 24
8. Butter Mocha Latte 24
9. Spinach and Feta Breakfast Wrap 25
10. Turkey Casserole 25
11. Blueberry-Banana Smoothies 26
12. Lime Chicken 27
13. Avocado and Bacon Egg Cups 27
14. Bagel Sandwich with Goat Cheese 28
15. Greek Yogurt Parfait 29
16. Almond-Apricot Granola 29
17. Smoked Salmon and Cream Cheese Roll-Ups: 30
18. Cauliflower Hash Browns 30
19. Green Smoothie Bowl 31
20. Coconut Tofu Curry 32
21. Southwest Breakfast Skillet 33
22. Cappuccino Chocolate Chip Muffin 33
23. Cherry Scones 34
24. Chicken Olive Artichoke Skillet 35
25. Zucchini and Bacon Egg Muffins 36
LUNCH 37
26. Grilled Chicken Caesar Salad 37
27. Shrimp Paella 37
28. Meatloaf 38
29. Spaghetti Squash-Sausage Casserole 39

30.	Easy Cheesy Bacon Quiche	40
31.	Shrimp Stir-Fry	40
32.	Zoodles Alfredo with Grilled Chicken	41
33.	Keto Caprese Salad with Balsamic Glaze	42
34.	Keto Beef and Broccoli Stir-Fry	43
35.	Cabbage and Beef Stir-Fry	43
36.	Keto-stuffed bell peppers	44
37.	Keto Lemon Garlic Butter Shrimp	45
38.	Shrimp and Avocado Lettuce Wraps	46
39.	Eggplant Lasagna	48
40.	Keto Garlic Parmesan Chicken	49
41.	Zucchini Noodles with Pesto and Cherry Tomatoes	49
42.	Keto Turkey and Avocado Lettuce Wraps	50
43.	Keto Spinach and Feta Stuffed Chicken	51
44.	Keto Spaghetti Squash with Meatballs	51
45.	Cauliflower and Bacon Cheese	52

DINNER 53

46.	Rice and Beef Soup	53
47.	Cheesy Tuna Casserole	55
48.	Slow-Cooker Pizza	56
49.	Holiday Lamb with Asparagus	57
50.	Zoodles with meatballs in an Italian sauce	58
51.	Curry with Spinach and Lamb	59
52.	Curried cauliflower soup	59
53.	Walleye Simmered in Basil Cream	60
54.	Italian Loaf of Meat	61
55.	Charleston Shrimp and Gravy over Grits	62
56.	Italian Style Roast in a Pot	63
57.	Cauliflower Rice and Luau Pork	64
58.	Chili Verde	64
59.	Pulled Pork with Apricots	65
60.	Buffalo Chicken Tacos	66
61.	French Style Potato Fries	66
62.	Cashew Chicken	67
63.	Chicken Vegetable soup	68
64.	Chicken Soup with Noodle	69
65.	Salmon accompanied with Spinach	69
66.	Tuna with Zoodles Casserole	70
67.	Broccoli and Mahi-Mahi Platter	71
68.	Surf and Turf	72
69.	Pork Chops	72
70.	Risotto with Seafood	73
71.	Tilapia with Chili-Garlic-Butter	74
72.	Asian-Inspired Tilapia	75

73.	Simple Salmon with Lemon	76
74.	Flank Steak with Horseradish and Garlic	76
75.	Asian Chicken Satay	77
76.	Beef Stir-up	78

SNACKS *79*

77.	Crust-Free Pizza	79
78.	Cilantro-lime Flounder	80
79.	Mashed Parmesan and Cauliflower Gravy	80
80.	Meatballs	81
81.	Sweet and Spicy Shrimp	82
82.	Zucchini and Beef-Stuffed Peppers	83
83.	Cheesy Spaghetti Squash	84
84.	Fresh Veggies with Herbs	85
85.	Prosciutto-Garlic Green Beans	85
86.	Pizza Casserole	86
87.	Veggie Burger	86
88.	Peppers Salsa	87
89.	Cheeseburger Casserole	88
90.	Deep Dish Pizza Crust	89
91.	Nachos	90
92.	Chicken Stir-Fry	90
93.	Cilantro-lime Flounder	91
94.	Jalapeño Poppers	92
95.	Zucchini Chips	92
96.	Buffalo Cauliflower Bites	93

Soup *94*

97.	Chicken Soup with Noodle	94
98.	Chicken Vegetable soup	95
99.	Curried cauliflower soup	96
100.	Rice and Beef Soup	96
101.	Cauliflower and Bacon Soup	97
102.	Thermion of Shrimp	98
103.	Broccoli and Cheddar Soup	99
104.	Chicken and Vegetable Soup	100
105.	Creamy Tomato Basil Soup	100
106.	Keto Spicy Cauliflower Soup	101
107.	Seafood Chowder	102
108.	Keto Cream of Asparagus Soup	102
109.	Mexican Chicken Avocado Lime Soup	103
110.	Roasted Red Pepper and Tomato Soup	104
111.	Thai Coconut Chicken Soup	104
112.	Egg Drop Soup	105
113.	Zucchini Soup	105
114.	Cobbler topped with Chicken Gravy	106

115.	Traditional Chicken-vegetable Soup	107
116.	Wild Mushroom and Thyme Soup	108
117.	Broccoli and Gold Potato Soup	109
118.	Mushroom Barley Soup	110
119.	Special Chicken Soup	111
120.	Lentil and Veggie Soup	112
121.	White Bean Soup with Orange	112
122.	Simple Tomato Basil Soup	113

DESSERT *114*

123.	Maple-Walnut Pots	114
124.	Blackberry-Thyme Granita	115
125.	Carrot Cookies with Chocolate Chip	115
126.	Banana-Oatmeal Cookies	116
127.	Marinated Berries	116
128.	Tofu Mocha Mousse	117
129.	Dessert Made with Grilled Mango	117
130.	Date Brownies	118
131.	Yogurt and Berry Freezer Pops	119
132.	Dark Chocolate and Cherry Trail Mix	119
133.	Pumpkin Pie Fruit Leathers	119
134.	Chilled Mango Yogurt Drink	120
135.	Wrapped with Almond Butter and Banana	120
136.	Cinnamon Pear Crisp	121
137.	Pumpkin Cakes Prepared in Ramekins	122

SALADS *123*

138.	Quinoa Salad	123
139.	Orange Salad	123
140.	Cucumber, Lemony Bulgur, and Lentil Salad	124
141.	Couscous Salad	124
142.	Green Salad with Oranges and Avocados	125
143.	Baked Beet Arugula Salad	126
144.	Chickpea and Tomato Salad	127
145.	Quinoa and Spinach Salad	127
146.	Tuna, Cashew, and Couscous Salad	128
147.	Avocado Salad with Roasted Carrots	129

A 30 DAYS MEAL PLAN *130*

CONCLUSION *132*

INTRODUCTION

Welcome to a culinary masterpiece designed for your health journey: "Dr. Nowzaradan's Keto Symphony Cookbook." Dr. Younan Nowzaradan, renowned for his expertise in transformative weight loss, invites you on a gastronomic adventure where delicious meets nutritious. This cookbook is not just a collection of recipes; it's a symphony of flavors harmonized to align with the principles of the ketogenic lifestyle.

In this culinary opus, Dr. Nowzaradan combines his extensive medical knowledge with the artistry of keto cuisine. Each page of this cookbook resonates with a passion for wellness, offering a symphony of low-carb, high-fat, and moderate-protein compositions that are as delightful to the taste buds as they are conducive to your health goals.

As you embark on this journey, expect a culinary crescendo featuring diverse recipes that cater to a spectrum of tastes and preferences. From succulent protein choices to vibrant, low-carb vegetables and decadent healthy fats, every ingredient plays a crucial role in the symphony of nutritional excellence. This cookbook isn't just about shedding pounds; it's about savoring the richness of life through the palate while nourishing your body.

No matter how much or how little experience you have with the ketogenic diet or the low-carb lifestyle, "Dr. Nowzaradan's Keto Symphony Cookbook" promises a delectable experience. Join us in turning your kitchen into a stage for wellness, where each recipe is a note in the grand symphony of your health journey. Let the culinary symphony begin, and may your health flourish as you indulge in the harmony of flavors curate by Dr. Nowzaradan himself.

Within these pages, discover culinary crescendos that range from hearty breakfasts to savory dinners and delightful desserts. Dr. Nowzaradan's expertly crafted recipes offer a symphony of taste and nutrition, guiding you toward a keto lifestyle that's not just transformative but a celebration of the artistry of healthy living.

"Dr. Nowzaradan's Keto Symphony Cookbook" is an invitation to savor culinary diversity on your keto journey. Immerse yourself in a gastronomic narrative where the vibrant colors of vegetables, the melodies of protein, and the harmonies of healthy fats create a symphony of taste unparalleled in the world of ketogenic cuisine. With each recipe, Dr. Nowzaradan extends his medical wisdom to your kitchen, providing not just a cookbook but a companion in your quest for a healthier you. This collection isn't about deprivation; it's a celebration of mindful, delicious choices that redefine your relationship with food, leading you towards the crescendo of well-being.

PART 1: Fundamental Knowledge

What You Need to Know About Diet

In concluding our exploration of "What is Dr. Nowzaradan's Keto Diet?" we've unveiled more than a dietary regimen; it's a philosophy of balanced living. Dr. Nowzaradan's approach to the ketogenic lifestyle is not just about shedding pounds; it's a transformative journey toward holistic well-being.

As you close this informational chapter, carry with you the understanding that the keto lifestyle isn't a temporary fix but a sustainable paradigm shift. It's a conscious choice to fuel your body with nourishing, low-carb alternatives while reveling in the rich tapestry of wholesome foods. Dr. Nowzaradan's insights extend beyond a diet plan; they're keys to unlocking a healthier, more vibrant version of you.

Embrace the knowledge that food is not just sustenance but a tool for empowerment. May your journey with Dr. Nowzaradan's keto principles be a continuous exploration of vibrant health, mindful choices, and a renewed appreciation for the harmony of nutrition and tasty. This is not just an endpoint; it's the commencement of a lifestyle where well-being is not just a goal but a daily commitment. Here's to your health, your journey, and the vibrant chapters yet to be written in the book of your well-lived life.

About The Diet

In unraveling the intricacies of "What is Dr. Nowzaradan's Keto Diet Plan?" we find ourselves immersed in a holistic approach to well-being crafted by the seasoned hands of a medical maestro. Dr. Younan Nowzaradan, renowned for his expertise in transformative weight loss, extends his guiding hand to usher us into the realm of ketogenic living.

At its core, Dr. Nowzaradan's keto plan is not merely a dietary protocol; it's a prescription for a sustainable, health-conscious lifestyle. This isn't a rigid set of rules; it's a flexible framework designed to cater to individual needs and preferences. The emphasis lies not just on shedding excess weight but on fostering a balanced, nutrient-rich diet that fuels the body while appeasing the taste buds.

The cornerstone of this keto symphony is a meticulous balance of macronutrients—a choreography of low-carb, moderate-protein, and healthy fat intake. Dr. Nowzaradan's approach prioritizes whole, unprocessed foods, urging us to relish the bounties of lean proteins, vibrant vegetables, and satiating fats.

Beyond the culinary components, Dr. Nowzaradan's plan is a call to mindfulness. Portion control becomes a practiced art, and hydration is not just a routine but a cornerstone of health. It's a plan that understands the individuality of each journey, acknowledging that success isn't just in the destination but in the daily choices we make.

As you embark on Dr. Nowzaradan's keto voyage, envision it not as a temporary diet but as a lifestyle tapestry where each meal is a brushstroke, coloring your canvas of well-being. It's a journey marked not only by pounds lost but also by the profound transformation of how we view and interact with food. Here's to the orchestration of health, the symphony of flavors, and the chapters of vitality yet to unfold in the narrative of your wellness journey.

The Benefits

Embarking on Dr. Nowzaradan's Keto Symphony Diet Plan opens a gateway to a myriad of health benefits, offering more than just a culinary adventure. As you delve into the symphony of flavors prescribed in the cookbook, the advantages extend beyond weight loss, presenting a holistic approach to well-being.

1. Sustainable Weight Loss: The cornerstone of Dr. Nowzaradan's keto approach is its efficacy in promoting sustainable weight loss. By restricting carbohydrate intake and relying on healthy fats and proteins, the body transitions into a state of ketosis, encouraging the utilization of stored fat for energy. By doing so, you may help yourself lose weight and lay the groundwork for healthy weight control in the future.

2. Enhanced Mental Clarity: The ketogenic diet is renowned for its cognitive benefits. By stabilizing blood sugar levels and providing a consistent source of fuel to the brain through ketone bodies, followers often report increased mental clarity and improved focus. This mental sharpness can positively impact daily productivity and overall well-being.

3. Stable Energy Levels: Unlike the energy swings associated with high-carb diets, Dr. Nowzaradan's keto plan guarantees a constant supply of energy. By relying on fats as a primary energy source, individuals experience sustained energy levels throughout the day, minimizing the notorious energy crashes often linked to carb-heavy meals.

4. Appetite Control and Reduced Cravings: The satiating nature of the keto diet, enriched with healthy fats and proteins, contributes to better appetite control. Individuals often report reduced cravings for sugary and processed foods, fostering a healthier relationship with eating and minimizing the likelihood of overindulgence.

5. Improved Metabolic Health: The keto lifestyle has been associated with improved metabolic markers, including enhanced insulin sensitivity and better blood sugar control. This can be particularly beneficial for individuals with insulin resistance or those at risk of metabolic disorders.

6. Heart Health Benefits: Healthy fats, such as olive oil and seafood that is high in omega-3 fatty acids, are emphasized in Dr. Nowzaradan's ketogenic diet, which is consistent with heart-healthy concepts. This can contribute to improved lipid profiles, including lower levels of triglycerides and increased levels of beneficial HDL cholesterol.

7. Stable Blood Sugar Levels: One of the standout benefits of the keto diet is its impact on blood sugar levels. By minimizing carbohydrate intake, the diet helps regulate blood glucose, which is particularly beneficial for individuals with diabetes or those aiming to prevent insulin resistance.

8. Anti-Inflammatory Effects: The ketogenic diet has a number of components that have anti-inflammatory characteristics. One of these components is omega-3 fatty acids, which may be found in nuts and fatty fish. There is a correlation between chronic inflammation and a variety of health problems, and the ketogenic diet has the ability to decrease inflammation, which may contribute to overall improved health.

9. Hormonal Balance: The keto diet can influence hormonal balance, particularly in women with conditions like polycystic ovary syndrome (PCOS). By stabilizing insulin levels and reducing inflammation, the diet may contribute to hormonal equilibrium, potentially addressing some symptoms associated with hormonal imbalances.

10. Enhanced Physical Endurance: For those engaged in physical activities, the keto diet offers benefits in terms of endurance. By utilizing fat stores efficiently, individuals on the keto diet may experience sustained energy during prolonged physical efforts, making it an attractive option for athletes and fitness enthusiasts.

11. Therapeutic Potential for Neurological Conditions: Beyond cognitive benefits, the keto diet has shown promise for certain neurological conditions, such as epilepsy. The diet's neuroprotective effects may extend to other neurological disorders, although consultation with a healthcare professional is crucial for personalized recommendations.

12. Support for Healthy Aging: Some research suggests that the keto diet might have implications for healthy aging by addressing factors linked to age-related cognitive decline. While more research is needed, the diet's influence on brain health hints at potential benefits for the aging population.

13. Hormesis and Cellular Repair: Hormesis, or mild stress, is a concept that the keto diet can activate. This may contribute to cellular longevity and resilience, potentially offering protective effects against certain age-related conditions.

14. Triglyceride Reduction: Triglycerides are a form of fat that may be present in the blood, and the ketogenic diet is known to lead to a drop in triglyceride levels. Triglyceride levels that are elevated are linked to an increased risk of cardiovascular disease, and the influence that the diet has on decreasing these levels adds to the health of the cardiovascular system for individuals.

15. Potential Cancer Therapeutic Effects: Emerging research explores the potential therapeutic effects of the keto diet on certain types of cancer. While more studies are needed, the diet's influence on metabolism and its anti-inflammatory properties are areas of interest in cancer research.

16. Hormonal Appetite Regulation: The keto diet has been shown to positively influence hormones that regulate appetite. By promoting a sense of fullness and reducing ghrelin, the hunger hormone, individuals may find it easier to adhere to calorie-appropriate portions, aiding in weight management.

17. Improved Skin Health: The ketogenic diet has helped some people with skin issues, including acne, feel better. The reduction in processed foods and sugars, coupled with the anti-inflammatory effects of the diet, can contribute to healthier skin.

18. Better Sleep Quality: Balancing blood sugar levels and reducing the consumption of stimulants like sugar and refined carbs can positively impact sleep quality. Many individuals on the keto diet report improvements in the duration and depth of their sleep.

19. Gastrointestinal Health: The keto diet's focus on whole, unprocessed foods, including fiber-rich vegetables, supports a healthy gut. This can contribute to improved digestion and may benefit individuals with certain gastrointestinal conditions.

20. Positive Impact on Mental Health: While more research is needed, some studies suggest a potential link between the keto diet and improved mental health. Stable blood sugar levels and the diet's impact on neurotransmitters may play a role in mood regulation.

Dr. Nowzaradan's Keto Symphony Diet Plan

Welcome to a transformative journey of health and flavor with Dr. Nowzaradan's Keto Symphony Cookbook. This diet plan is crafted to harmonize with the principles outlined by Dr. Nowzaradan, blending the richness of ketogenic cuisine with a practical approach to sustainable weight loss and improved well-being.

Meal Schedule:

1. **Breakfast (8:00 AM):**
   - Keto Omelets with spinach, tomatoes, and feta cheese.
   - Bulletproof coffee with MCT oil for sustained energy.

2. **Snack (10:30 AM):**
   - Handful of mixed nuts (almonds, walnuts, and macadamias).

3. **Lunch (1:00 PM):**
   - Grilled chicken or tofu salad with avocado, greens, with olive oil dressing.

4. **Snacks (4:00 PM):**
   - Greek yogurt with chia seeds and a few raspberries.

5. **Dinner (7:00 PM):**
   - Baked salmon or cauliflower rice stir-fry with assorted vegetables.
   - Steamed broccoli drizzled with butter.

6. **Evening Snack (9:30 PM):**

- o   Herbal tea or bone broth for relaxation.

Guidelines:

- **Snack Smart:** Opt for keto-friendly snacks to curb cravings, emphasizing whole, minimally processed foods.
- **Hydration:** Aim to drink at least 3 liters of water throughout the day. Herbal teas and black coffee are also encouraged.
- **Variety is a key:** Rotate protein sources (poultry, fish, and tofu) and incorporate a rainbow of vegetables for a variety of nutrients.
- **Smart Fats:** Consume foods that include healthy fats, such as nuts, avocados, and olive oil, to promote satiety and to help the body enter a state of ketosis.

Remember, this diet plan is a starting point. Adjust the amount of your portions and the foods you choose to eat depending on your own requirements and preferences. Consult with a healthcare professional for personalized advice, and enjoy the symphony of flavors and health benefits that Dr. Nowzaradan's Keto Cookbook brings to your table.

Recommended Food List

Proteins:

1. **Chicken:** grilled chicken breast baked chicken thighs.
2. **Fish:** fat-fish such as salmon, tuna, trout, and others
3. **Lean Meats:** Turkey, lean cuts of beef, pork tenderloin.
4. **Tofu is a** versatile plant-based protein source.

Vegetables:

1. **Cruciferous Vegetables:** Brussels sprouts, Broccoli, Cauliflower.
2. **Leafy greens:** Swiss chard, kale, lettuce, and spinach.
3. **Low-Carb Veggies:** Zucchini, asparagus, green beans, and bell peppers.
4. **Avocado is a** nutrient-dense source of healthy fats.

Fats:

1. **Olive Oil:** Extra virgin olive oil is used for cooking and dressings.
2. **Nuts:** almonds, walnuts, and macadamias.
3. **Seeds:** chia seeds, flaxseeds, and pumpkin seeds.
4. **Avocado Oil:** Ideal for high-heat cooking.

Dairy:

1. **Cheese:** Feta, mozzarella, cheddar, and cream cheese (in moderation).

2. **Greek Yogurt:** Opt for plain, unsweetened varieties.
3. **Butter:** grass-fed butter for cooking and flavor.

Beverages:
1. **Water:** Stay well-hydrated throughout the day.
2. **Herbal Tea:** Chamomile, peppermint, and green tea.
3. **Coffee:** black coffee or with a splash of unsweetened almond milk.
4. **Bone broth is a** nourishing and satisfying option.

Snacks:
1. **Berries:** limited amounts of raspberries, strawberries, and blackberries.
2. **Snacking on hard-boiled** eggs is a quick and easy way to get your protein fix.
3. **Pork Rinds:** A crunchy, low-carb alternative to chips.
4. **Cheese Sticks:** portable and satisfying.

Condiments:
1. **Olive Oil Dressing:** Mix with vinegar or lemon juice for salads.
2. **Mayonnaise:** Look for sugar-free, keto-friendly options.
3. **Mustard** adds flavor without adding sugar.
4. **Hot Sauce:** Ads spice without extra calories.

Remember, individual nutritional needs vary, so adjust quantities based on your specific requirements. If you are considering making large changes to your diet, you should always get the advice of a dietician or a healthcare expert. Dr. Nowzaradan's Keto Symphony Cookbook encourages a diverse, nutrient-rich approach to keto living, ensuring a symphony of flavors on your journey to improved health.

Foods to Avoid

In adherence to Dr. Nowzaradan's keto principles, certain foods are best left off your plate to maximize the benefits of a ketogenic lifestyle. Steer clear of the following:

High-Carb Foods:

1. **Grains:** wheat, rice, oats, and other high-carb grains.
2. **Legumes:** beans, lentils, and chickpeas.
3. **Starchy Vegetables:** Potatoes, sweet potatoes, and corn.
4. **High-Sugar Fruits:** Bananas, mangoes, and grapes.

Processed Foods:

1. **Sugary Snacks:** Candies, cookies, and other high-sugar treats.
2. **Sweetened Beverages:** soda, fruit juices, and sugary energy drinks.
3. **Processed Meats:** pre-packaged sausages with added sugars.

High-fat, non-keto oils:

1. **Vegetable Oil:** Corn, soybean, and other highly processed vegetable oils.
2. **Tran's fats:** foods containing partially hydrogenated oils.

Dairy with Added Sugars:

1. **Flavored yogurts:** those with added sugars and fruit.
2. **Sweetened Milk Alternatives:** Flavored almond or soy milk with added sugars.

Condiments with Hidden Sugars:

1. **Ketchup** is often high in sugar.
2. **Barbecue Sauce:** Many commercial varieties contain added sugars.

Hidden Carbs:

1. **Processed foods:** Check labels for hidden carbs in sauces and dressings.
2. **Alcohol:** Limit consumption, as some alcoholic beverages can be high in carbs.

Artificial Sweeteners:

1. **Aspartame** is found in some diet sodas and sugar-free products.
2. **Sucralose:** Sucralose is another artificial sweetener to be cautious about.

By avoiding these non-keto-friendly foods, you pave the way for a more effective and sustainable ketogenic journey with Dr. Nowzaradan's Keto Symphony Cookbook. Always consult with a healthcare professional or a dietitian to tailor your diet to your specific health needs and goals.

PART 2: The Recipes

BREAKFAST

1. Chia Seed Pudding

What we need:

- 1 cup of almond milk
- 1 tablespoon crushed coconut
- ¼ cup chia seeds
- Berries for topping

Cooking method:

1. Almond milk and Chia seeds should be mixed together in a dish.
2. After giving it a good stir, let it rest for ten minutes.
3. Before covering it and placing it in the freezer for the night, give it a couple more stirs before covering it.
4. Perform a thorough stir on it first thing in the morning to break up the particles that may have formed throughout the previous night.
5. Before serving, garnish each portion with shredded coconut and fresh berries.

2. Avocado and Bacon Egg Cups

What we need:

- 4 eggs
- 2 avocados, halved and pitted
- 4 slices of bacon, minced
- Pepper-salt to taste
- Chopped chives for garnish

Cooking method:

1. Get your microwave ready for 190 degrees Celsius. Cut out a well in the avocado by taking out a little of the meat. The well will serve as a mold for all the egg.
2. In a baking dish, arrange the avocado halves in a single layer. Use a small spoon to crack an egg into each side of the avocado. Make sure the yolk fits into the well.

3. You can season with pepper-salt to your liking. On top, there should be bacon crumbles.
4. Put it in the microwave for 12 to 15 minutes, or until the eggs are the consistency you want.
5. Dress it up with chopped chives, and then serve.

3. Omelet

What we need:
- Canola oil (1 tsp)
- 2 sprigs parsley
- Onion (2 tbsp)
- 1 whole egg
- Green bell pepper, diced (2 tablespoon)
- 2 egg whites
- Shredded hash browns (2 tbsp)
- Soy milk (1 tbsp)

Cooking method:
1. In a pan that does not stick, take the canola oil and heat it over medium heat.
2. Place the chopped onion and parsley leaves into the cooker and fry them until the onion is translucent and has a scent that is pleasing to the senses.
3. In a bowl, include the whole egg, the egg whites, and the soy milk. Carefully combine all of the elements until they are completely mixed into the mixture.
4. After adding the egg to the pan, spread it out with a spatula around the surface of the pan until it fully covers the whole surface. The eggs should be allowed to cook for a few minutes, until the sides begin to stiffen.
5. On one side of the omelet, put the diced green bell pepper and chopped hash browns.
6. Making a half-moon shape with the filling in the middle of the omelet, flip the other portion of the omelet over gently using a spoon.
7. Use the spoon to gently press down on the egg to make sure the fixings are spread out evenly.
8. Cook the omelet for another minute or two, until the eggs are done and the fixings are hot.

9. Put the egg on a platter, garnish with the parsley sprig, and serve the dish while it is still hot.

4. Chicken with Green Beans

What we need:

- 1 teaspoon of vegetable oil
- 2 finely minced garlic cloves
- ¾ cup green beans that have been diced
- ½ tablespoon of raw pine nuts, four ounces of boneless, skinless chicken breast, sliced into three uniform strips, and no salt.
- ¼ of a teaspoon of grated black pepper
- ½ teaspoon of chopped fresh basil leaves

Cooking Method:

1. After bringing the oil to a boil in a medium-sized cooker and placing it over a medium heat source, the next step is to fry the garlic for one to two minutes.
2. The second step is to combine the green beans and pine nuts, and then continue to boil the mixture for an average of three minutes, or until the green beans have become flexible and can be easily punctured with a knife.
3. Place the chicken in the pan, and once it is cooked, season it with the pepper and the basil.
4. Tend to the meat for five minutes per side while it cooks.
5. Turn the chicken over after three to five minutes, when the temperature on the inside of the chicken reaches 165 degrees Fahrenheit. And mix the green beans and pine nuts. Dish up.

5. Broccoli and Pasta

What we need:

- 8 ounces of uncooked pasta made from whole wheat
- 1-ounce container of cherry tomatoes
- 2 and a third cups of low-sodium vegetable broth
- 1 and a half cups of natural peanut butter
- 3 tablespoons of vinegar
- 1 tablespoon of olive oil, extra-virgin

- 1 tenth of a teaspoon of toasted sesame oil
- 1 and a half teaspoons of low-sodium soy sauce
- 1 clove of garlic, diced up
- 3.5 cups of broccoli florets, which is about 1 pound

Cooking Method:

1. Place a big pot filled with water over heat and bring to a boil.
2. Follow the instructions on the back of the pasta package to cook the pasta until it is firm to the bite.
3. In the meantime, combine the tomatoes with the broth, peanut butter, vinegar, canola oil, sesame seed oil, soy sauce, and garlic in a big cooker set over high heat.
4. Continue to cook, turning the mixture often, as long as the tomatoes burst.
5. As soon as the pasta is finished cooking, add the broccoli and let it simmer for a few minutes.
6. Within the next three minutes, bring the mixture to a simmer. After draining the cooking liquid, add the sauce and mix everything together until it is evenly coated.
7. Take service.

6. Waffle Sandwich

What we need:

- 1 (1.33-ounce) solidified multigrain waffle
- 2 tablespoons cream cheese, mollified
- 2 teaspoons dark-colored sugar
- Ground cinnamon (¼ teaspoon)
- 1 tablespoon of raisins
- 1 tablespoon hacked pecans, toasted

Cooking method:

1. Toast waffles as per bundle headings.
2. Blend cream cheese, dark sugar, and cinnamon until very well mixed. Spread the cream cheese blend over the waffles. Sprinkle with raisins and pecans.
3. Cut the waffle down the middle. Sandwich waffle parts together with filling inside.

7. Berry Chia Pudding

What we need:
- 1 cup chia seeds
- 1 ½ cups unsweetened almond milk
- ½ teaspoon vanilla essence
- 1 tablespoon erythritol
- ½ cup mixed berries

Cooking method:
1. It is recommended that chia seeds, almond milk, vanilla extract, and sweetener be mixed together in a bowl before usage.
2. After thoroughly combining the ingredients, it should be placed in the refrigerator for at least two hours or longer.
3. Chia pudding should be stirred just before serving to ensure that it has a smooth consistency.
4. Place the chia pudding in a serving dish or glass, and then layer it with a mixture of berries.
5. If you want, you may finish it off with a spoonful of Greek yogurt that is unsweetened.
6. Savor a breakfast that is both reviving and satisfying.

8. Butter Mocha Latte

What we need:
- Unsalted butter (2 tablespoons)
- 1 ¼ cups unsweetened cashew milk (or hemp milk if sans nuts)
- 2 tablespoons unsweetened cocoa powder, in addition to extra for topping (discretionary)
- 2 tablespoons swerve confectioners-style sugar or a proportionate measure of fluid or powdered sugar
- 3 tablespoons hot fermented decaf coffee or other solid blended decaf espresso, whipped cream, for trimming (discretionary)
- Immersion blender

Cooking method:
1. Pour the unsalted butter in a cooker over high heat, mixing until the butter froths and dark-colored spots start to show up around 5 minutes; this is browned butter. If utilizing butter-seasoned coconut oil, heat the oil just until softened.

2. Decrease the warmth to medium and gradually rush in the cashew milk; it will sizzle as you add it to the browned butter. Stir in the cocoa powder and sugar. Whenever wanted, embed an infusion blender and mix until the blend takes the shape of a foamy latte, around 1 minute.

3. Empty the coffee into a giant cup. Include the hot milk blend and mix well. Serve promptly, decorated with whipped cream and a sprinkle of unsweetened cocoa powder, whenever wanted.

9. Spinach and Feta Breakfast Wrap

What we need:

- 2 eggs
- 1 cup fresh spinach, minced
- 2 tablespoons of creamy cheese
- Salt and pepper to taste
- 1 tablespoon of olive oil for cooking

Cooking method:

1. Salt and pepper should be added to the eggs after they have been whisked in a bowl.
2. Place the olive oil in a saucepan and turn the heat to medium. Heat the olive oil to a sizzle over medium heat.
3. Prepare the pan by adding chopped spinach and stirring it until it wilts.
4. Pour the eggs that have been whisked over the spinach.
5. There is feta cheese sprinkled on top of the eggs.
6. After the eggs have reached the desired consistency, fold the combination into a wrap.
7. Serve while still heated.

10. Turkey Casserole

What we need:

- Ten fresh eggs
- ½-ounce turkey sausage
- One mug of no-sugar-added salsa
- One mug of heavy cream
- Salt and pepper

- One mug of Mexican cheese blended
- One teaspoon of chili powder
- Half a teaspoon of garlic powder
- ½ teaspoon cumin

Cooking method:

1. Heat a skillet and cook the sausage.
2. When it isn't pink, blend in salsa and seasonings.
3. Put out from warmth.
4. In a dish, beat the milk and eggs as needed.
5. Mix the pork as well as the cheese, and stir.
6. Prepare a Casserole with a coconut-oil-based cooking spray.
7. Pour in the casserole and close the cover.
8. Heat on low for five hours, or if you want to eat sooner, on high for 2–½ hours.

11. Blueberry-Banana Smoothies

What we need:

- 1.5 ounces of water
- 1 liquid ounce of blueberries
- ½ cup of silken tofu
- 1 and a half ready bananas of medium size, cut into pieces
- Greek yogurt, nonfat, plain, 1 (5.30 oz.) section

Cooking method:

1. To make this, put all the elements in a mixer and mix until smooth.
2. Serve it cool.

12. Lime Chicken

What we need:

- One skinless, boneless chicken breast of four ounces' worth
- ⅛ cup of lime juice that has been freshly squeezed
- ⅛ cup of fresh cilantro that has been diced
- 2 cloves of garlic, finely chopped
- 1 tablespoon of mustard Dijon
- ¼ of a tablespoon of olive oil
- ¼ teaspoon of grated chili peppers
- 1 eighth of a teaspoon of new black pepper
- When required, salt

Cooking Method:

1. Get a baking sheet hot in the microwave—350 degrees Fahrenheit is the recommended temperature.
2. Put all of the parts in the food grinder and give them a few pulses, except the chicken, until they are well blended.
3. Set the chicken breasts in a glass baking dish that is suitable for the microwave and is 7 inches by 11 inches. After 15 minutes, or for as long as six hours, after coating the chicken in the marinade you created, cover it in plastic wrap and store it in the refrigerator.
4. Put the dish in the microwave and bake it without a lid for 18 to 20 minutes, or until a thermometer with a rapid reading reaches 165 degrees Fahrenheit. Dish up.

13. Avocado and Bacon Egg Cups

What we need:

- 2 large avocados, halved and pitted
- 4 slices of cooked bacon, crumbled
- 4 large eggs
- Chopped chives for garnish
- Salt to taste
- pepper to taste

Cooking method:

1. Preheat the microwave throughout the heating process.

2. In order to create a well for the egg, first cut every avocado in half and then remove a little portion from each side of the avocado.
3. To prevent the avocados from toppling over, it is recommended that they be put on a baking sheet.
4. Begin by inserting 1 egg into each side of the avocado.
5. In addition to seasoning with salt and pepper, crumbled bacon should be sprinkled on top.
6. Bake for twelve to fifteen minutes, or until the eggs have reached the desired level of doneness.
7. To finish, sprinkle some chopped chives on top before serving.

14. Bagel Sandwich with Goat Cheese

What we need:
- ½ cup (4 ounces) goat cheddar, disintegrated
- 4 ounces cream cheese, mollified
- 2 tablespoons of honey
- 1/3 cup hacked toasted pecans
- 1 cinnamon-raisin twirl small bagel, split and toasted
- ¼ cup red Anjou pear, unpeeled and meagerly cut

Cooking method:
1. Consolidate the initial three ingredients in a little bowl. Mix in pecans.
2. Spread 1 tablespoon of goat cheddar uniformly onto the cut sides of the bagel.
3. Spot pear cuts on the base portion of the bagel. Supplant the bagel top.
4. Spread and chill, staying spread for as long as a week.

15. Greek Yogurt Parfait

What we need:

- 1 cup Greek yogurt (unsweetened)
- ¼ cup of fresh raspberries
- ¼ cup of blueberries
- 2 tablespoons crushed nuts walnuts
- 1 tablespoon of chia seeds
- Stevia or erythritol for sweetness (optional)

Cooking method:

1. Combining Greek yogurt with sugar, if preferred, in a bowl is the first step.
2. Create a parfait by layering Greek yogurt, blueberries, raspberries, and chopped almonds in a shallow dish or glass.
3. Keep piling on layers until you've reached the very top.
4. To enhance the texture and nutritional value of the dish, sprinkle chia seeds on top.
5. Before serving, store in the fridge for a minimum of thirty minutes to get the best results.

16. Almond-Apricot Granola

What we need:

- 2 cups antiquated, moved oats
- 1 cup cut almonds
- Honey (½ cup)
- Oil (2 tablespoons)
- Cinnamon (¼ teaspoon)
- Cooking splash
- 2 cups dried apricots, coarsely cleaved

Cooking method:

1. Set the microwave temperature to 300 degrees.
2. Consolidate the oats and almonds in a dish. Combine honey and oil in a little pot. Heat up to boiling, blending sporadically. Mix in cinnamon and salt; pour honey blend over oat blend, hurling until oats are altogether covered.

3. Spread the oat blend uniformly onto a 17 x ½ x 1 inch container covered with cooking spray. Prepare at 300° for 35 to 38 minutes, blending at regular intervals, until the granola is brilliantly dark-colored. Let it cool on a heating sheet. Blend in the apricots. Store it in a sealed pot.

17. Smoked Salmon and Cream Cheese Roll-Ups:

What we need:
- 4 slices of smoked salmon
- 2 tablespoons of cream cheese
- 1 tablespoon capers
- Fresh dill for garnish
- Lemon wedges for serving

Cooking method:
1. The slices of smoked salmon should be laid out.
2. Each slice should have a very thin coating of cream cheese spread on it.
3. The capers should be distributed equally on the cream cheese.
4. Create a rollout of the salmon slices, and then use toothpicks to attach them.
5. Add some fresh dill as a garnish.
6. It is recommended to serve slices of lemon on the side.

18. Cauliflower Hash Browns

What we need:
- 2 cups crushed cauliflower
- ¼ cup almond flour
- ¼ cup grated cheese
- 2 large eggs
- ½ teaspoon garlic paste
- Salt to taste
- Olive oil for cooking
- pepper to taste

Cooking method:

1. Crushed cauliflower, almond flour, cheese, egg, garlic paste, pepper, and salt should be combined in a bowl and then stirred together.
2. Shape the ingredients into patties of a smaller size.
3. Get the olive oil to a heat that is somewhere in the middle of a skillet.
4. Cook the cauliflower patties until they have a golden brown color on both sides throughout the cooking process.
5. As a side dish or as a foundation for eggs that have been poached or fried, serve.

19. Green Smoothie Bowl

What we need:
- 1 cup of minced spinach
- ½ avocado
- ½ cup almond milk
- 1 scoop milk powder
- 1 tablespoon of chia seeds
- Ice cubes (optional)

Toppings: sliced strawberries, unsweetened coconut flakes, and chopped nuts

Cooking method:
1. To make a smooth smoothie, blend together powder milk, chia seeds, almond milk, spinach, and avocado until smooth.
2. If they wish, add ice cubes and mix the mixture once more.
3. The smoothie should be placed in a bowl.
4. For garnish, sprinkle some chopped nuts, coconut flakes, and sliced strawberries on top.

20. Coconut Tofu Curry

What we need:

- 1 and a half pounds of tofu that has a firm texture
- 2 tablespoons of olive oil, measured out in a tablespoon
- 1 cup of chopped frozen onion from the grocery store
- 5 cups worth of frozen vegetables, to be cooked in a stir-fry
- 1 teaspoon of spicy paste, with more to your liking
- 1 can of coconut milk that is less thick and has a volume of 14 ounces
- 1 milliliter of the juice of a lime that has just been squeezed from fresh limes
- 1 milliliter of vegetable broth with decreased sodium content

Cooking Method:

1. After allowing the block of tofu to drain, divide it into two rectangular pieces by cutting it lengthwise along its equator.
2. Arrange them so that they are parallel to one another in a number of layers of fresh paper towels, and then place something substantial on top of the paper towels, like a book or a frying pan. Clear the space.
3. Using a knife that is very sharp, cut your tofu cubes into squares that have an outer length of one inch.
4. Place the oil in a big cooker and warm it over moderately high heat until it shimmers. When it reaches the shimmering stage, you may then add the tofu.
5. When it is heating for the following five minutes, do not stir it in any way so that the bottom may get a golden brown color.
6. After about four to five minutes, turn the food and keep cooking it until it is golden. Position the tofu so that it is facing up on the serving piece that you are utilizing.
7. Put the onion in the pan that you've been using to heat up the oil that's left behind, and then fry the veggies in that pan. Get ready for a delay of two minutes. Continue cooking for an additional minute after you've added the curry paste to the dish.
8. Using a ladle, pour the coconut milk into the bowl. After it has achieved a rolling simmer, decrease the heat to a boil and keep cooking for an additional 5 minutes. The lime juice goes on top once it has been poured.
9. Place the tofu back into the cooker and keep cooking it over medium-high heat, flipping it often, until it is completely opaque all the way through. You can assist with this.

21. Southwest Breakfast Skillet

What we need:

- 2 eggs
- ¼ cup chopped bell peppers (mix of colors)
- ¼ cup chopped tomatoes
- ¼ cup chopped onions
- ¼ cup grated cheese
- 1 tablespoon of olive oil
- ½ avocado, sliced
- Fresh cilantro for garnish
- Salt to taste
- pepper to taste

Cooking method:

1. In a skillet, bring the olive oil to a medium temperature.
2. Include tomatoes, onions, and bell peppers in the dish. To soften the meat, sauté it.
3. As the veggies cook, crack eggs into the pan and allow them to cook with the vegetables.
4. Sprinkle the eggs with the shredded cheddar cheese over it.
5. Cover the cooker and continue cooking the eggs until they reach the desired level of doneness and the cheese has melted.
6. For seasoning, use salt and pepper.
7. The dish is finished off with avocado slices and freshly cut cilantro.

22. Cappuccino Chocolate Chip Muffin

What we need:

- Cooking shower
- 1 and 3/4 cups low-fat heating blend
- Sugar (½ cup)
- ½ cup of high-temperature water
- 2 tablespoons of instant coffee granules
- Canola oil (¼ cup)
- One enormous egg

- Half a cup of semisweet chocolate is smaller than regular chips.

Cooking method:
1. Preheat the broiler to 400°.
2. Put ½ paper biscuit cup liners in the biscuit cups; coat them with cooking spray.
3. Put the mixture into dry measuring cups, being careful to keep the cups level with the blade. Whisk the heating mixture and sugar together in a medium bowl.
4. Join ½ cups of high-temperature water and espresso granules, blending until the espresso breaks down. Consolidate the oil and egg, mixing with a whisk; mix in an espresso blend. Add the espresso blend to the heating blend, mixing just until sodden. Blend in chocolate-scaled-down chips.
5. Spoon the player into arranged liners. Heat it for 20 minutes at 400°F or until the biscuits spring back when contacted softly. Expel the biscuits from the container quickly and put them on a line rack. Serve warm.

23. Cherry Scones

What we need:
- 9 ounces of flour (around 2 cups)
- Salt
- Sugar (¼ cup)
- Heating powder (one and a half teaspoon)
- ¼ cup chilled, unsalted margarine
- 3/4 cup dried tart fruits, slashed
- Fat-free buttermilk (3/4 cup)
- Cooking shower
- 1 tablespoon turbaned sugar (discretionary)

Cooking method:
1. Bring the microwave down to 425°.
2. Estimate or softly spoon flour into dry measuring cups; then, smooth with a blade.
3. Consolidate the flour, salt, sugar, and powder in a big dish, mixing admirably with a whisker. Then cut in the spread, utilizing a good blender, until the blend looks like coarse supper. Blend in fruits.
4. Include buttermilk and almonds separately whenever wanted, mixing just until damp.

5. Mix the butter onto a daintily floured surface and massage gently multiple times, including with floured hands. Structure the mixture in an 8-inch pan on a prepared sheet covered with a cooking sheet.

6. Cut the butter into 10 wedges, slicing into but not through the combination. Coat the top of the butter with cooking spray. Sprinkle with turbinate sugar whenever desired.

7. Keep the preparation sheet on a rack on the stove. Heat it at 425° for 20 minutes or until brilliant.

24. Chicken Olive Artichoke Skillet

What we need:
- Extra-virgin olive oil, two tablespoons
- 4 chicken thighs with the bones in but without the skin
- Split ¼ teaspoons of salt
- ½ teaspoons of new black pepper, divided
- 1 low-sodium can of chopped tomatoes
- 1 can, drained
- ¼ cup water
- 1 can of quartered artichokes, drained
- ¼ cup of pitted Kalamata olives
- ¼ cup of finely chopped fresh parsley

Cooking Method:
1. The microwave should be preheated at 350 degrees Fahrenheit, and a baking sheet should be placed inside.

2. In a microwave-safe cooker that is suitable for direct use in the microwave, over medium-high heat, the oil should be brought to a boil. This pan may be used anywhere in the microwave. The chicken should be seasoned with 14 teaspoons of salt and pepper.

3. Cook the chicken for roughly two to three minutes on both sides, so that it has a golden exterior, using a heat setting that is set to medium. Put it on the plate you have available.

4. Deglaze any browned bits left in the pan by adding the crushed tomatoes and a little water.

5. After the remaining salt has been dissolved, add the artichoke hearts, olives, pepper, and any residual salt. Be sure to thoroughly combine.

6. Put the chicken on the skillet, and then transfer it to the microwave for the last 20 minutes of cooking. Take it out of the microwave and set it aside. Serve with the parsley sprinkled on top.

25. Zucchini and Bacon Egg Muffins

What we need:

- 4 large eggs
- ½ cup grated zucchini
- 3 slices of boiled crumbled bacon
- ¼ cup grated cheese
- Chopped chives for garnish
- pepper to taste
- Salt to taste

Cooking method:

1. Prepare a muffin tray by greasing it and preheating the microwave.
2. After the eggs have been whisked in a dish, they should be seasoned with salt and pepper before being served.
3. Grate the zucchini, crumble the bacon, and add the shredded mozzarella to the mixture.
4. This mixture should be poured into muffin cups.
5. Bake the egg muffins for fifteen to eighteen minutes, or until they have reached the desired consistency.
6. To finish, sprinkle some chopped chives on top before serving.

LUNCH

26. Grilled Chicken Caesar Salad

What we need:

- Crispy bacon bits (optional)
- 2 boneless, skinless chicken breasts
- Caesar dressing (keto-friendly)
- 2 tablespoons of olive oil
- Cherry tomatoes, halved
- Salt to taste
- Romaine lettuce, chopped
- pepper to taste
- Parmesan cheese, shaved

Cooking method:

1. The chicken breasts should be seasoned with salt and pepper.
2. Place a grill pan over medium-high heat, and heat the olive oil in the pan.
3. Chicken breasts should be grilled for roughly six to eight minutes each side until they are fully done.
4. Before slicing, let the chicken rest for a little.
5. Combine romaine lettuce that has been cut, cherry tomatoes, and Parmesan cheese that has been shaved in a big bowl.
6. On top is grilled chicken that has been cut.
7. Apply a Caesar dressing that is suitable for ketogenic diets, and if you want, add some crispy bacon pieces on top.

27. Shrimp Paella

What we need:

- 1½ pounds of big shrimp that have been cleaned and peeled
- ½ can of drained diced tomatoes with less salt
- Diced half of an onion and two glasses of water
- 1 cup of whole-grain rice
- 3 teaspoons of olive oil
- ⅛ teaspoon of salt

- 1 teaspoon of black pepper, grated

Cooking Method:

1. After pouring oil and shrimp into a pan, bring the temperature of the oil to a low-medium level.
2. After the shrimp have been fried, allow them to cook for two to three minutes on each side before transferring them to a platter.
3. The same quantity of oil that is left over should be brought to a boil in the same skillet by heating it over a medium setting that is the same as the one that was used before.
4. The onion should be stir-fried for around three to five minutes.
5. In a large mixing bowl, combine the rice that has been cooked, the water, the tomato products that have been chopped, the paprika, the pepper, and the salt.
6. You should allow it to boil for the whole specified time.
7. The flame should be reduced to a simmer, and it should remain there. Keep the cover on and continue cooking for twenty-five to thirty minutes or until all of the water has been absorbed.
8. Eliminate the pan from the heat source. Following the completion of the mixing process, the shrimp should be served.

28. Meatloaf

What we need:

- Two eggs
- One pound of ground pork
- One teaspoon of paprika
- One pound of ground turkey
- 2 cups chopped onion
- One tablespoon of coconut oil
- Two teaspoons of red pepper flakes
- ½ cups of almond flour
- One tablespoon of garlic powder
- Six teaspoons of Italian seasoning
- Use salt and pepper.

Cooking method:

1. After pouring oil into a pan, bring the temperature of the oil to a low-medium level.

2. When the temperature is warm, combine the onions and cook them until they become translucent.

3. Take it off the heat immediately. Eggs, spices, and almond flour, and whisk to combine in a dish.

4. Add the meat along with the onions, and then mix everything together with clean hands. Take the shape of a loaf.

5. A spray that contains coconut oil should be used to grease your slow cooker.

6. Ensure that the top of the loaf is flat and that there is a minimum of a half-inch of space between the meat and the edges of the slow cooker before placing the loaf into the slow cooker.

7. Within close proximity to the lid of the cooker. Steam on high heat for 180 minutes, or until the temperature of the meat reaches 150 degrees.

8. The loaf should be allowed to rest in the cooker for fifteen to thirty minutes after it has been cooked, with the lid removed and the stove turned off. This will ensure that the loaf is substantial and does not crumble.

9. Consume!

29. Spaghetti Squash-Sausage Casserole

What we need:
- 1 pound of pork breakfast sausage
- 3 cups of cooked spaghetti squash
- ¼ teaspoon red pepper flakes
- ½ teaspoon garlic powder
- 8-ounces shredded cheddar cheese
- ¼ cups almond flour
- Four beaten eggs
- ¼ cups heavy cream
- Use salt and pepper as needed.

Cooking method:
1. Prepare breakfast sausage in a pan until it loses its pink color and takes on a seared appearance.

2. First, combine the spaghetti squash and flour in a dish, and then add the sausage.

3. The next step is to combine the spices, cream, cheese, with eggs in another bowl.

4. The spaghetti squash combination should be placed in a slow cooker that has been oiled.
5. The egg mixture should be poured over it, and then it should be placed next to the lid of the pan.
6. Raise the temperature to a low level for five to seven hours.
7. Serve when still hot!

30. Easy Cheesy Bacon Quiche

What we need:
- 1 cup of heavy cream
- 6 beaten eggs
- 8-ounces shredded mozzarella cheese
- 1 teaspoon of onion powder
- 1 tablespoon of grass-fed butter
- 6 pieces of cooked, chopped bacon
- Use pepper and salt as needed.

Cooking method:
1. Put the eggs, cheese, cream, and spices on a plate and mix them together.
2. Grease the slow cooker with the butter, and make sure to leave any excess butter inside.
3. After the egg mixture has been poured into the slow cooker, the diced bacon should be added on top. Within close proximity to the lid of the dish.
4. The next step is to cook it for four hours at a low temperature.

31. Shrimp Stir-Fry

What we need:
- 1 bell pepper, sliced
- Chopped green onions
- 1 pound shrimp, peeled and deveined
- 2 cups of broccoli florets
- 3 cloves garlic, minced
- 2 tablespoons of sesame oil
- 2 tablespoons soy sauce (or tamari for gluten-free)

- 1 tablespoon ginger, grated
- 1 teaspoon erythritol)
- 1 tablespoon of rice vinegar
- Sesame seeds for garnish

Cooking method:

1. In order to properly prepare the sesame oil, it is essential to heat it in a cooker over medium flame.
2. An amount of time ranging from one to two minutes should be spent sautéing grated ginger and chopped garlic.
3. Add the shrimp to the stir-fry after they have reached a pink color and become opaque.
4. Then add the bell pepper and broccoli and carry on to fry the mixture until the vegetables are tender.
5. Combine the rice vinegar, erythritol, and soy sauce in a small dish and swirl them together until they are well mixed.
6. After the sauce has been poured over the other ingredients, the shrimp and vegetables should be stirred in the sauce.
7. To end, sprinkle some sesame seeds and green onions over the top of the dish.

32. Zoodles Alfredo with Grilled Chicken

What we need:
- 2 chicken breasts, grilled and sliced
- 2 zucchinis, spiralizer into noodles
- ½ cup grated Parmesan cheese
- 1 cup heavy cream
- 3 cloves garlic, minced
- 2 tablespoons of butter
- Salt to taste
- Fresh parsley for garnish
- pepper to taste

Cooking method:

1. Melting butter takes place in a pan that is heated to a medium temperature. After the garlic has matured and developed its scent, sauté it.

2. After the heavy cream has been brought to a simmer, grated Parmesan cheese should be mixed into the sauce until it reaches the desired consistency.
3. When seasoning food, use both salt and pepper.
4. After the zucchini noodles have been well coated with the Alfredo sauce, toss them in the sauce.
5. To serve, add a cut piece of chicken that has been grilled on top of the dish that has been completed.
6. Garnish with some fresh parsley that has been mixed in.

33. Keto Caprese Salad with Balsamic Glaze

What we need:

- 1 cup cherry halved tomatoes
- 1 cup crushed fresh mozzarella
- 2 tablespoons olive oil
- pepper to taste
- Fresh basil leaves
- 1 tablespoon balsamic glaze
- Salt to taste

Cooking method:

1. To prepare the cherry tomatoes and fresh mozzarella for serving, arrange them in a certain arrangement on a tray that is designed for presentation.
2. It is recommended that you insert some fresh basil leaves into the dish after you have placed the mozzarella and tomatoes in the center of the dish.
3. After the preparation of the salad has been finished, immediately sprinkle it with extra virgin olive oil and balsamic glaze over the top.
4. You are free to season it with salt and pepper in accordance with your own personal tastes.
5. One may be certain that this dinner, which is appropriate for ketogenic diets, will be an option that will revitalize you.

34. Keto Beef and Broccoli Stir-Fry

What we need:

- 1 lb. flank steak, thinly sliced
- 1 tablespoon sesame oil
- 3 tablespoon soy sauce (or tamari for gluten-free)
- Green onions, chopped
- 1 tablespoon grated ginger
- 2 tablespoon olive oil
- 2 cups of broccoli florets
- 2 minced garlic cloves
- 1 teaspoon erythritol (or keto-friendly sweetener)

Cooking method:

1. For optimal results, marinating sliced steak in a combination of erythritol and soy sauce in a container is recommended.
2. To unleash the scent of the garlic and ginger, heat the oil in a cooker and fry them so that they release their perfume.
3. Continue to cook the steak until it has a browned appearance after you have added the steak that has been marinated.
4. After placing the broccoli in the pan, stir-fry it until it reaches the desired consistency.
5. Onion and sesame seeds should be used as garnishes, and next a trickle of sesame oil should be spread on the top.

35. Cabbage and Beef Stir-Fry

What we need:

- 1 small cabbage, chopped
- 1 bell pepper, thinly sliced
- 1 onion, minced
- 1 pound of minced beef
- 2 cloves garlic, minced
- Green onions for garnish
- 2 tablespoons soy sauce or coconut aminos

- 1 teaspoon crushed ginger
- 1 tablespoon sesame oil
- Pepper-salt to taste

Cooking method:

1. To brown the ground beef, place it in a big pan or wok and roast it over low-medium heat. Any fatty accumulation should be removed.
2. Garlic and onions should be diced, while cabbage and bell peppers should be sliced.
3. All of these ingredients should be thrown into a skillet. To get a crisp-tender texture, cook in a skillet.
4. When you are cooking the meat and vegetables, add some soy sauce or coconut aminos.
5. Salt, pepper, ginger, and sesame oil should then be used to season the dish.
6. Stirring the components together will help to combine them.
7. Continuously whisk the mixture for a further three to five minutes to guarantee that everything is uniformly coated and cooked.
8. Green onions, chopped, should be used as a garnish.
9. Meat and cabbage that have been stir-fried should be served as soon as possible.

36. Keto-stuffed bell peppers

What we need:

- 1 teaspoon Italian seasoning
- Fresh parsley for garnish
- 1 cup of cauliflower rice
- 4 large bell peppers, halved
- 1/2 cup diced tomatoes
- 1 lb. ground beef
- Salt to taste
- 1 cup shredded cheddar cheese
- ½ cup tomato sauce (sugar-free)
- 2 cloves garlic, minced
- pepper to taste

Cooking Method:

1. A temperature of 375 degrees Fahrenheit (180 degrees Celsius) should be reached in the microwave.
2. To brown the ground beef, place it in a skillet with crushed garlic and cook it over medium heat.
3. A mixing bowl should be used to combine the diced tomatoes, tomato sauce, and cauliflower rice.
4. Before serving, season with pepper, salt, and Italian seasoning.
5. After the bell peppers have been split in half, place the mixture inside each of them.
6. The top should be topped with some shredded cheddar cheese.
7. To get a tender texture, the peppers should be cooked for 25–30 minutes.
8. Finally, right before serving, garnish with fresh parsley.

37. Keto Lemon Garlic Butter Shrimp

What we need:
- Fresh parsley for garnish
- 4 tablespoon unsalted butter
- 1 teaspoon dried thyme
- Zest and juice of 1 lemon
- 1 pound shrimp, peeled and deveined
- Salt to taste
- 3 cloves garlic, minced

Cooking Method:
1. Butter is melted in the pan when the temperature is set to medium, which is the temperature on the stovetop.
2. Sauté the garlic when it has been added, and continues to do so until it acquires an aromatic character.
3. In the beginning, before adding the shrimp to the dish, you should make sure that they are pink and opaque.
4. At the same time, the lemon zest, lemon juice, and dried thyme have to be mixed in a single container.
5. When it comes to seasoning the food, pepper and salt are both essential ingredients.
6. As a final touch, brush some fresh parsley on top of the meal just before it is served.

38. Shrimp and Avocado Lettuce Wraps

What we need:

For the shrimp:

- 1 pound of large shrimp, peeled and deveined
- 2 tablespoons of olive oil
- 2 cloves garlic, minced
- 1 teaspoon paprika
- Pepper-salt to taste
- Lime wedges for serving

For the avocado filling:

- Large iceberg or butter lettuce leaves, washed and dried
- 2 ripe avocados, diced
- Pepper-salt to taste
- ½ red diced onion
- ¼ cup fresh chopped cilantro
- 2 teaspoon of lemon sap

Cooking method:

1. The shrimp should be peeled and deveined before being combined with crushed garlic, olive oil, paprika, salt, and pepper in a big dish containing the shrimp.
2. First, get a skillet ready by heating it over a flame that is rather low.
3. After placing the shrimp in the cooker with the seasoning, cook them for two to three minutes on both sides until they are cooked and opaque, whichever comes first.
4. Lime juice that has been freshly squeezed should be used to lightly toss the shrimp.
5. To prepare the avocados, red onion, jalapeño, cilantro, lime juice, salt, and pepper, separate the ingredients and mix them together.
6. Gently mixing each component together is the best way to combine them all.

Lettuce wraps assembly Cooking method:

1. Using a spoon spread the avocado concoction over the lettuce leaves in every direction.
2. Include a couple of shrimp that have been grilled on top of the avocado mixture.
3. When you are ready to serve the shrimp lettuce wraps with avocado, prepare a serving plate.

4. Include more lime wedges in the serving.

Caprese Chicken Skewers

What we need:

- Cherry tomatoes
- 3 tablespoons of Olive oil
- 1 pound of chicken breast, cut into bite-sized cubes
- Wooden skewers, soaked in water
- Fresh mozzarella balls
- Balsamic glaze
- Fresh basil leaves
- Pepper-salt as taste

Cooking method:

1. Cut some chicken into cubes and put them in a bowl with some pepper and salt.
2. Before serving, let it sit in the marinade for at least fifteen minutes.
3. On wooden skewers, alternately thread the chicken marinade, cherry tomatoes, mozzarella balls, and basil leaves. Skewer the ingredients in a circular manner.
4. Place the skewers on a grill or barbecue and cook them over medium heat for roughly five to seven minutes per side. This will ensure that the chicken is not pinker in the center and has a lovely brown color.
5. Balsamic glaze should be used to bast the skewers after they have been arranged on a plate where they will be served.
6. These Caprese Chicken Skewers are ideal for sharing or eating alone since they are keto-friendly and full of flavor. I highly recommend these.

39. Eggplant Lasagna

What we need:

- Fresh rosemary leaves for garnish
- 2 large eggplants, thinly sliced lengthwise
- Pepper-salt to taste
- 1 teaspoon dried oregano
- 1 cup grated Parmesan cheese
- 1 cup of ricotta cheese
- 1 pound of ground beef
- 2 crushed garlic cloves

- 1 cup grated cheese
- 2 cups of sugar-free marinara sauce

Cooking method:

1. Put the pieces of eggplant on a roasting tray and season them with pepper-salt. This will get the eggplant ready to be cooked.

2. For drying them off, you may use kitchen towels. In a pan over low heat, cook the ground beef. Any fatty accumulation should be removed.

3. Combine the meat that has been browned with the pepper, salt, dried oregano, and garlic that has been minced in a basin.

4. Take a separate dish, the ricotta, mozzarella, and Parmesan cheeses should be combined and blended together.

5. A baking dish should be prepared with the eggplant pieces, meat mixture, cheese combination, and marinara sauce arranged in the order listed above. Continue the procedure by adding another layer of cheese on top of the previous one.

6. The mozzarella should be baked in the microwave for 35 to 40 minutes in order to ensure that it is melted and bubbling.

7. As a garnish, feel free to use fresh basil leaves.

8. After the lasagna has had some time to cool down, transfer it to plates using a ladle.

40. Keto Garlic Parmesan Chicken

What we need:

- 4 boneless, skinless chicken breasts
- 2 teaspoons garlic powder
- pepper to taste
- 2 tablespoons of olive oil
- Fresh parsley for garnish
- 1/2 cup grated Parmesan cheese
- 1/2 cup almond flour
- Salt to taste

Cooking Method:

1. Preheat the microwave to a temperature of 190 degrees Celsius (375 degrees Fahrenheit).

2. The following components should be mixed together in a bowl: garlic powder, salt, pepper, almond flour, and Parmesan cheese.
3. Applying the mixture, coat each chicken breast in its own unique manner.
4. The olive oil should be warmed in a pan that may be placed in the microwave.
5. Through the process of searing, make sure that the chicken is browned on both sides.
6. Once you have moved the pan to the microwave, once you have placed it there, roast it for twenty to twenty-five minutes.
7. To finish, sprinkle some fresh parsley on top just before serving.

41. Zucchini Noodles with Pesto and Cherry Tomatoes

What we need:
- Salt to taste
- 1 cup cherry tomatoes, halved
- 4 medium-sized zucchinis, spiralizer
- ½ cup homemade or store-bought pesto (keto-friendly)
- pepper to taste
- ¼ cup pine nuts, toasted

Cooking Method:
1. In a pan, zucchini noodles should be boiled until they are just a little pliable but not completely mushy.
2. The cherry tomatoes should be added to the pan, and the cooking process should be continued for another two to three minutes.
3. Incorporate the pesto into the mixture until it is spread uniformly throughout the mixture.
4. Seasoning food with pepper and salt is a must.
5. Immediately before serving, sprinkle the top with pine nuts that have been toasted.

42. Keto Turkey and Avocado Lettuce Wraps

What we need:

- 1 teaspoon of cumin
- 1 lb. ground turkey
- 1 tablespoon of olive oil
- 1 teaspoon chili powder
- 1 avocado, sliced
- Salt to taste
- Iceberg lettuce leaves
- pepper to taste
- Salsa (sugar-free) for topping

Cooking Method:

1. The ground turkey should be browned in the pan while the olive oil begins to warm up. This should take place while the pan is being heated.
2. It is recommended that chili powder, cumin, freshly ground black pepper, and salt be used in order to complement the dish.
3. To ensure that the turkey mixture is evenly distributed among the leaves of the iceberg lettuce, it is advised that a spoon be used.
4. Additionally, it is suggested that slices of avocado and salsa be placed on top of the dish.
5. The use of these items as wraps is a possibility.

43. Keto Spinach and Feta Stuffed Chicken

What we need:

- 2 teaspoons of Italian seasoning
- Olive oil for cooking
- 4 boneless, skinless chicken breasts
- 1/2 cup crumbled feta cheese
- Salt to taste
- 1 cup fresh spinach, chopped
- 2 tablespoons of cream cheese
- pepper to taste

Cooking Method:

1. A temperature of 375 degrees Fahrenheit should be reached in the microwave.
2. A bowl should be used to combine the spinach, feta cheese, cream cheese, Italian seasoning, salt, and pepper. The ingredients should be mixed.
3. It is recommended that a pocket be carved into each individual chicken breast.
4. Attempt to pack the pockets with the spinach and cheese mixture that you have placed inside of them.
5. The olive oil should be warmed in a pan that may be placed in the microwave.
6. It is important to sear the chicken on both sides as well.
7. Once you have moved the pan to the microwave, once you have placed it there, roast it for twenty to twenty-five minutes.

44. Keto Spaghetti Squash with Meatballs

What we need:

- Fresh parsley for garnish
- pepper to taste
- 1 cup of sugar-free marinara sauce
- 1 medium spaghetti squash, halved and seeds removed
- 1/4 cup grated Parmesan cheese
- 1 lb. ground beef or turkey
- 1 teaspoon Italian seasoning
- Salt to taste

Cooking Method:

1. When the spaghetti squash is ready, place it in the microwave and bake it until it can be easily pierced with a fork.
2. A grill pan is the method of choice for cooking ground beef or turkey, since this is the suggested method.
3. In addition to the addition of more salt and pepper, it is suggested that Parmesan cheese, Italian spice, and Marinara sauce be included in the dish.
4. In order to create strands of spaghetti squash, scrape the squash with a fork and then drain the component.
5. A topping for the meal may be made by using the meatball mixture as the ingredient.

6. Add some fresh parsley that has been incorporated into the dish as a garnish.

45. Cauliflower and Bacon Cheese

What we need:

- 1 medium cauliflower, cut into florets
- 1/2 lb. bacon, cooked and crumbled
- 1 teaspoon Dijon mustard
- Chopped chives for garnish
- 2 tablespoons of cream cheese
- Salt to taste
- 2 cups shredded sharp cheddar cheese
- ½ cup heavy cream
- pepper to taste

Cooking Method:

1. In the course of the cooking process, it is anticipated that the cauliflower will become soft.
2. Heavy cream, cream cheese, Dijon mustard, salt, and pepper should be mixed together in a saucepan and whisked until the mixture is completely smooth. This will result in a consistency that is absolutely smooth.
3. While the shredded cheddar is being incorporated into the mixture, it should be allowed to melt.
4. The combination of crumbled bacon, cheese sauce, and cauliflower is something that is recommended to be used.
5. Adding some chopped chives is a good idea if you want to garnish it.

DINNER

46. Rice and Beef Soup

What we need:

- Extra-lean ground beef (½ pound)
- Beef broth, prepared (1 cup)
- Black pepper
- One sweet onion, chopped
- Thyme, chopped (1 teaspoon)
- Minced garlic
- White rice, uncooked (½ cup)
- ½ cup green beans
- One celery stalk, chopped
- Water

Cooking method:

1. Put the pan on a low temperature and add the minced meat. The meat needs to be cooked for a certain amount of time until it turns brown.
2. Reduce the amount of excess fat.
3. After some time has passed, the onion and garlic should be added to the pan. You should cook them for around three minutes.
4. After that, add the rice, celery, beef broth, and water. Bring the water to a boil, and then turn the heat down. Keep the temperature at a low simmer for about a half an hour.
5. After that, toss in the thyme and the legumes, and then maintain the pot on a low heat for approximately three more minutes.
6. Remove them from the burning environment.
7. Pepper should be used to season them.

Thermion of Shrimp

What we need:

- A total of ¼ more cups of softened ghee or unsalted spread are to be added at the very end if using pig skins, for a total of ½ cups of fat if using margarine.
- 2 cups of chopped fresh shiitake
- ¼ cups of chopped onions
- Large shrimp (about 30 per pound), peeled and deveined

- Chicken bone stock, homemade or store-bought; enough to fill a cup
- 1 package of aged cream cheese (about 8 ounces)
- 3/4 smashed cup of cheddar
- Pork skins, smashed and divided into ½ cups (optional)
- ½ cups of Parmesan cheddar cheese ground

Cooking method:

1. Turn the grill up to high heat.
2. Over moderate heat, melt ½ cup of ghee in a cast-iron pan until it is liquid. Sauté the mushrooms and onions in batches until the mushrooms are a deep, rich color, about 5 minutes.
3. Mix in the shrimp, and then carry on cooking for another three minutes so the shrimp are opaque all the way through.
4. The next step is to mix the cream of mushroom soup and the cream cheese in a grinder and pulse so that soft before adding it to the skillet.
5. Blend in the cheddar and 1 cup of the crushed pork skins. Pour the mixture into a 9-by-9-inch square goulash dish.
6. Parmesan cheese and the remaining ½ cups of smashed pig skins (if used) should be spread over the goulash's peak. If you're using pig skins, pour ¼ cup of melted ghee on top.
7. Warm the cheddar for 2–4 minutes in the microwave, or until it reaches the desired texture, before grilling.
8. You may keep extra things cold for up to four days in the refrigerator's sealed section.
9. Warm in a dish that has been heated on the stove for 4 minutes, or until the food is fully cooked.

47. Cheesy Tuna Casserole

What we need:

- 1 tablespoon ghee or unsalted margarine (or coconut oil or fat if sans dairy), in addition to extra for lubing the dish
- 1 clove of garlic, crushed to glue
- 3 (6-ounce) jars of fish, depleted
- 1 ½ cups cauliflower florets, cubed
- 1 tablespoon chopped onion
- ½-inch pieces
- 1 cup slashed dill pickles
- 1/3 cups cream cheddar (Kite Hill brand cream cheddar style spread if sans dairy), mellowed
- 2 tablespoons mayonnaise, natively constructed or locally acquired
- ½ teaspoons of fine ocean salt
- ¼ teaspoon ground dark pepper
- 1 cup destroyed sharp cheddar (precludes dairy-free) Sliced green onions, for embellishment Chopped crisp parsley, for topping
- Cherry tomatoes, divided or quartered, contingent upon the size, for embellishment

Cooking method:

1. Prepare the broiler to 375 degrees Fahrenheit. Prepare a ghee-oiled dinner plate that measures 11 inches by 7 inches.
2. In a skillet over high heat, melt one teaspoon of butter. Cooking the onions one batch at a time for a few minutes until their color becomes transparent is the proper procedure to follow. Continue frying the mixture for one more minute after adding the garlic. Take it out of the pan and place it someplace safe.
3. Transfer the veggies to a bowl suitable for medium-sized mixing. Add the fish, cauliflower, and pickles to the veggies, along with the cream cheese, salt, mayonnaise, and pepper, and mix to incorporate everything.
4. Add the fish mixture to the goulash-lubricated plate. If you're using cheddar, crumble some of it over the top. Cook until the cauliflower is soft and the top is caramelized, about 20 minutes.
5. Remove from heat and let set for 5 minutes. Green onions, parsley, and cherry tomatoes should be used as garnishes before serving.

6. This meal is at its finest when served fresh, but any leftovers may be stored in a container that is hermetically sealed and placed in the refrigerator for up to three days.

7. It should be warmed for three minutes in a dish that has been prepared and placed in a broiler that has been preheated to 350 degrees Fahrenheit.

48. Slow-Cooker Pizza

What we need:

- 2 kg of ground beef from grass-fed cattle
- Two cups of shredded cheddar
- ¼ ounces of sugar-free marinara sauce for your spaghetti
- Pepper-salt
- Two cups' worth of mozzarella cheese that has been shredded
- One teaspoon's worth of garlic paste

Cooking method:

1. Preheat the pan in order to get it ready.
2. Incorporate meat, garlic, and the other spices that you choose.
3. Once the brown color has been removed from the meat, drain any excess oil that has formed in the pan.
4. To grease your slow cooker, use a product that includes coconut oil and spray it with that product.
5. Put the meat in the base of the cooker, and then mix the cheese and sauce to the top portion, which should be adjacent to the cover. The lid should be on the pan at this point.
6. It required a low-and-slow cooking method that lasted for a total of four hours.
7. Enjoy!

49. Holiday Lamb with Asparagus

What we need:

- 3-pound bone-in leg of lamb
- 5 cups of fresh asparagus
- Three minced garlic cloves
- ½ teaspoon dried thyme
- ¼ cups of fresh, chopped mint
- ¼ cup of water
- Two tablespoons of grass-fed butter
- ½ teaspoon dried parsley
- Pepper-salt as needed.

Cooking method:

1. Once it has been dried, the lamb should be rubbed all over with a combination that includes salt, thyme, parsley, and pepper.
2. To make the butter easier to work with, microwave it in a big dish.
3. Include lamb and cook it for around five minute's total, cooking it on both sides.
4. Put the lamb on top of the element that is heating up the microwave.
5. Garlic and mint should be added, depending on the situation.
6. Pour in water.
7. At a relatively close distance to the cover of the pan.
8. Ten hours of preparation should be done on a low-heat setting. When the specified period of time has passed, take the lamb out of the microwave and put it to the side.
9. After you have completed the previous step of returning the lamb to its original position on top of the veggies in the slow cooker, the next step is to add the asparagus.
10. Next to the cover of the pot, and then continue to let it simmer for another two hours after that.
11. Serve!

50. Zoodles with meatballs in an Italian sauce

What we need:

- 1 medium-twisted zucchini
- 32 oz. beef stock
- 1 tablespoon of sliced onion 2 ribs of chopped celery
- 1 carrot that's been chopped
- 6 minced garlic cloves
- 1 pound crushed beef
- 1 ½ teaspoons of garlic
- ½ cups of shredded parmesan cheese
- 1 big egg
- ½ teaspoon pepper
- ½ troy ounces of each
- dry minced onions; Himalayan pink salt
- 1 tablespoon of each:
- Italian spice, dried oregano Italian seasoning

Cooking method:

1. Start by turning on the slow cooker and adjusting the temperature to its lowest setting.
2. Put the carrot, zucchini, onion, celery, tomato, garlic salt, and beef stock into the slow cooker. Put the cap back on.
3. Combine the egg, parmesan, parsley, Italian spices, pepper, ground beef, sea salt, oregano, garlic paste, and onion powder in a mixing dish or another container. Combine, and then roll into thirty golf-ball-sized meatballs.
4. Warm the oil over medium flame. While it is heated, add the meatballs that have been browned and throw them into the slow cooker.
5. Prepare on a low setting while keeping the lid on for a period of six hours.

51. Curry with Spinach and Lamb

What we need:

- 1 pound of lamb, cut into cubes
- 1 pound of spinach that is still fresh
- One can of tomatoes weighs in at ¼.5 ounces.
- One onion that has been minced
- Two cloves of garlic that have been minced
- Two tablespoons of fresh ginger that has been minced
- Cumin, to taste, two tablespoons
- Garam masala, in the amount of two teaspoons
- Salt to taste

Cooking method:

1. Place everything in the dish, and then whisk it well. The dish should be placed near the pan's lid.
2. Reheat on low for a total of eight hours overnight.
3. Try it out, and add some salt if you think it needs it!

52. Curried cauliflower soup

What we need:

- 3 cups of water
- One small cauliflower
- Unsalted butter (one teaspoon)
- One onion, chopped
- Sour cream (½ cup)
- Curry powder (two teaspoons)
- Garlic, minced (2 teaspoons)
- Cilantro, chopped (three tablespoons)

Cooking method:

1. Utilizing a big pan and heating it over a moderate setting will ensure that the butter is thoroughly melted.

2. Cooking the garlic and onion for around three minutes should be sufficient time.
3. Within a large bowl, stir together the cauliflower, curry powder, and water.
4. Once all of the ingredients have come to a full boil, decrease the flame to a low and continue cooking.
5. Maintain a low simmer for around twenty minutes.
6. Put the components in a grinder and prepare them so the mixture is silky fluid.
7. Repeat the process of transferring the soup to the saucepan.
8. Mix in the finely chopped coriander as well as the sour cream.

53. Walleye Simmered in Basil Cream

What we need:
- ¼ cups of overwhelming cream (or full-fat coconut milk if sans dairy)
- ¼ cups of new basil leaves, in addition to extras for enhancement
- 2 tablespoons ghee or unsalted spread (or coconut oil if sans dairy), partitioned
- ½ cups cleaved onions
- 1 clove of garlic, crushed to glue
- 1 pound of walleye fillets, cleaned and cut
- Salt to taste
- ¼ teaspoon ground dark pepper
- ¼ cup fish or chicken bone soup, handcrafted or locally acquired cherry tomatoes, cut down the middle, for enhancement

Cooking method:
1. Get a grinder and add the cream and basil. Blend or process until the leaves of basil are no longer mixed with the cream.
2. Put a pan on the burner to get the temperature up. After dissolving the ghee in the hot pan, add the onions and garlic and continue to sauté them for an additional two minutes, or until the onions have turned translucent.
3. Pepper-salt should be used to season the fish pieces. Place the fish in the skillet, and add the stock and cream of basil. Stir to combine. Cook the fish, uncovered, for seven minutes, or until the flesh is opaque all the way through and chips easily.

54. Italian Loaf of Meat

What we need:

- A pound and a half of extra-lean ground sirloin
- Spray for non-stick cooking surfaces or an olive oil-filled spray bottle
- 2 big eggs
- 1 c. grated zucchini—approx. 1 medium
- 4 minced cloves of garlic
- ½ ounces of fresh of each
- Parsley that has been cut very finely (+) more for topping
- Parmesan cheese that has been grated
- 3 tablespoons balsamic vinegar
- 2 tablespoons of chopped dried onion or onion powder

Topping what we need:

- 2 tablespoons of finely chopped fresh parsley
- ¼ cents worth of each:
- Shredded mozzarella cheese, approx. 2-3 slices
- Tomato sauce/ketchup
- An oval slow cooker with a capacity of 6 quarts is recommended for use.

Cooking method:

1. Use cooking spray on the interior of the pot and cover it with aluminum foil.
2. Mix all of the fixings together, but do not include the topping ingredients. The consistency of the mixture will be runny. Form it into a loaf that is elongated in shape, and place it on a sling.
3. Create a sling for removing the dish from the slow cooker by using sheets of aluminum foil that are sufficiently long to wrap around the dish.
4. Make sure the cap is tight. You can choose to cook on a medium flame for three hours or low for six hours. Take the cooker off the power about fifteen minutes prior to the cooking cycle. Take off the lid, and then add the toppings.
5. Keep the main course out of the oven for another 5–10 minutes. Utilizing the metal strips, take it out of the saucepan. Before serving, place onto a serving dish and garnish with the chopped parsley.

55. Charleston Shrimp and Gravy over Grits

What we need:

- 3 pieces of bacon in strips
- 2 tablespoons of ghee or margarine that has not been salted
- 1 green ringer pepper, slashed
- ½ cups of onions cut into dice
- 1 clove of garlic, either finely chopped or pulverized to a paste.
- 1 pound of huge shrimp, peeled and deveined, numbering maybe about 30
- 2 tablespoons of fine-grained salt from the ocean
- ½ tablespoons of dark pepper that has been ground
- For each dish, you will need ½ cups of chicken bone stock, either homemade or

Cooking method:

1. Warm a cooker with oil over medium flame and mix the bacon. Sauté for about four moments or until the bacon is as crispy as you like it. Take it out of the frying pan and put it away in a location where it won't be damaged. The drippings should be saved in the pan for use at a later time.

2. Turn the heat down to medium once you have added the ghee to the pan that was previously using the bacon drippings as the cooking medium. After adding the onions and ringer pepper to the pan, sauté the mixture for approximately five minutes or until the onions have reached the desired level of tenderness. After adding the garlic, keep the pot on low heat for another minute while it simmers.

3. Pepper-salt should be used to season the shrimp. After adding the shrimp to the cooker, increase the temperature to medium and continue sautéing while continuously mixing the ingredients for about four minutes, or until the shrimp are opaque and no longer translucent.

4. The shrimp should be transferred to a heated plate using an open-ended spoon and then stored in a secure location.

5. While maintaining medium-high heat, pour the stock into the pan and use a whisk to work it into the base of the pan to deglaze it.

6. At this time, remove the pan from the heat, add the shrimp to the sauce, and stir to coat. The fluids should be heated until they have reached the desired level of thickness.

7. The shrimp should be served over a bed of keto cornmeal, and the crumbled bacon should be sprinkled on top.

56. Italian Style Roast in a Pot

What we need:

- Two cups of hearty beef broth
- Carrots, chopped, for two cups
- One finely minced onion
- 1 pound of tomatoes, crushed
- Chuck roast, boneless, weighing three pounds
- Tomato paste with no added sugar, one tablespoon
- Three cloves of garlic, minced
- Exactly one tablespoon of Italian seasoning that is salt-free
- Nutmeg, ground: 1/8 teaspoon
- To taste, add pepper-salt.

Cooking method:

1. Regardless of whether or not the meat has already been chopped, cut it into smaller pieces.
2. Place it in the saucepan that you normally use for the stew.
3. Utilize items such as carrots, onions, garlic, and spices in the dish you're preparing using your recipe.
4. Mix in some paste, some canned tomatoes, and some chicken stock, then stir to combine all of the ingredients.
5. Mix well before applying.
6. At a distance that is not too far from the lid of the pan.
7. To get it ready to eat, put it in a cooker with a lid and simmer it on a low setting for a total of eight hours.
8. Serve and enjoy! When it was time to tend to the meat, we got to work.

57. Cauliflower Rice and Luau Pork

What we need:

- 3 pounds Roast pork weighing
- Salt to taste
- 2 teaspoons of the liquid from the hickory
- 4 individual pieces of bacon
- 5 individual cloves of garlic
- 3 cups Rice made with cauliflower
- A quarter of a teaspoon's worth of garlic paste
- 2 teaspoons of chicken stock

Cooking method:

1. When you are finished arranging the bacon in the bottom of the slow cooker, sprinkle the garlic cloves in an equal layer over the top of it.
2. After it has been prepared, the roast should be seasoned before being put in the slow cooker.
3. It is necessary to include the hickory liquid in the combination.
4. After cooking on high for the first six hours of the total cooking time, steam for the last two hours of the process.
5. It is strongly suggested that the cauliflower be steamed.
6. Include them in the mixture that is now being reduced to a powder in the food processor.
7. It is appropriate to serve both at the same time.

58. Chili Verde

What we need:

- 2.2 kg of pork
- 3 teaspoons of chopped coriander
- 5 whole cloves of garlic
- 1 tablespoon cilantro
- There should be 3 tablespoons of butter.
- 1 and a half cups of salsa

- 0.25 salts

Cooking method:

1. Put the butter in the crock pot and turn it down to the smallest setting.
2. Along with the chopped cilantro, you also need to include a total of three tablespoons and four cloves of garlic.
3. It is necessary to make use of a pan in order to finish frying the remaining garlic and cilantro.
4. Make use of a pan while preparing the meat.
5. After doing so, the next step is to place the meat inside the slow cooker.
6. The meal is ready for the salsa to be added to it.
7. Check to ensure that all of the constituents are well mixed together.
8. Cook for a total of eight hours while maintaining a very low temperature.

59. Pulled Pork with Apricots

What we need:

- Three kg of lean pork
- 1 cup barbecue sauce
- 6 ounces of dried apricots are included in this ingredient.
- 10 kg of an apricot spread that does not include any sugar and does not include any
- A solitary onion with a moderate flavor

Cooking method:

1. After that, you should put the meat in the slow cooker.
2. The onions should be added after the barbecue sauce, spread, and apricots have been mixed together.
3. Prepare over very low heat for 11 hours.

60. Buffalo Chicken Tacos

What we need:

- 1,500 grams of chicken that has had the bones and skin removed but is otherwise boneless and skinless.
- The amount of butter should be equal to three tablespoons.
- 1 cup buffalo sauce

Cooking method:

1. Place each component into the pressure cooker in the order listed.
2. Prepare over low heat for a period of five hours.
3. Shred the chicken into pieces before cooking.

61. French Style Potato Fries

What we need:

- Pepper-salt
- Sweet potatoes are skinned and sliced very thinly.
- Olive oil
- Optional seasonings, such as paprika, garlic paste, or cayenne pepper, for added flavor

Cooking method:

1. Get the microwave ready by preheating it to 400 degrees Fahrenheit.
2. Set the potato fries in a massive basin and mix the combined oil also salt to the bowl. Make sure to cover the fries evenly so that they turn out crispy.
3. To give the fries more flavor, season them with salt, pepper, and whatever herbs you choose, keeping in mind that the sweet potatoes already have a distinct fragrance.
4. Season the sweet potato fries and lay them out in one layer on the roasting sheet that has been prepared. Leave a space between each fry to let it crisp up.
5. Cook the French fries in the microwave for about 22–28 minutes, turning them once halfway through the cooking process, until they are light golden in color and crisp.

62. Cashew Chicken

What we need:

- 1 cluster of green onions
- 1 chopped yellow bell pepper and 1 chopped celery branch
- 3 tablespoons of coconut oil
- 2 cups of thighs without bones or skin
- 2 tablespoons of finely chopped, peeled, and rinsed ginger
- 3 cups of stock made from chickens
- Black pepper
- 2 milligrams of arrowroot flour
- 1 teaspoon salt
- 1 cup of chopped, salted nuts
- 4 garlic cloves, chopped up

Cooking method:

1. Chopping scallions and other green and white ingredients
2. A weakling is best prepared by patting it dry, slicing it into 2-inch pieces, and seasoning it with pepper-salt.
3. Get a pan hot over high heat.
4. The chicken should be cooked for 5 minutes while the oil is flowing and being stirred. Head over to the trash can.
5. 5. Toss the celery around for about 7 minutes, so that the peppers, garlic, ginger, red-pepper chips, bell pepper, and scallion whites are soft together in a pan and stir continuously.
6. Vegetables in a bowl, then the soup is mixed with arrowroot flour and sauce.
7. Turn down the heat and simmer until reduced, occasionally stirring up trouble.
8. Mix in the chicken, scallion greens, cashews, and liquids.

63. Chicken Vegetable soup

What we need:

- Unsalted butter
- Ground black pepper
- ½ diced sweet onion
- Chicken stock, one cup
- Thyme, chopped (one teaspoon)
- Two celery stalks, chopped
- Water
- Minced garlic (2 teaspoons)
- Cooked chicken breast, chopped (2 cups)
- One carrot, diced
- Parsley (two tablespoons)

Cooking method:

1. You may melt the butter in the pan you have by choosing a heat setting that is somewhere in the middle.
2. After adding the garlic and onion, continue to cook for approximately three more minutes.
3. After a certain amount of time has passed, you will want to add carrots, water, celery, and chicken stock to the pot.
4. The soup has to be brought to a simmer at this point.
5. Decrease the temperature to a low setting and keep going to steam at a low simmer for around thirty minutes.
6. After that, the thyme should be added, and the soup should be allowed to boil for an additional two minutes.
7. Pepper is the perfect condiment to use for seasoning them.
8. Before serving, garnish with chopped, fresh parsley.

64. Chicken Soup with Noodle

What we need:

- Chicken broth (1 ½ cups)
- Salt
- Cooked chicken (1 cup)
- Water
- Black pepper
- Carrot (¼ cup)
- Poultry seasoning (¼ tsp)
- Uncooked egg noodles (2 oz.)

Cooking method:

1. Place the water as well as the broth inside the slow cooker, and then adjust the temperature so that it is as low as it can go.
2. Salt, black pepper, and poultry spice are not already included in them; thus, these three spices will need to be added to them before they can be used.
3. The preparation of the chicken requires a number of steps, two of which are the cutting of the carrot and the paring of the bird.
4. They should be put into the broth at the same time as the noodles if you want the best results.
5. Approximately twenty-five minutes should be set aside in order to carry out the cooking operation.
6. Keep the temperature at a gentle simmer for around five minutes.

65. Salmon accompanied with Spinach

What we need:

- 2 kg of salmon, either fresh or thawed from frozen
- ½ teaspoons worth of garlic paste
- ½ ounces of spinach that is still fresh
- Two lemons, sliced each
- ¼ ounces of vegetable stock
- ½ teaspoons of dried onion flakes

- As required, pepper-salt may be used.

Cooking method:

1. Place the spinach in the slow cooker and pack it in as tightly as possible to make room.
2. Pepper, onion powder, salt, and garlic paste should be applied to all surfaces of the fish before seasoning.
3. Place the fish on top of the greens on the serving dish.
4. Arrange the pieces of lemon over the salmon, and then pour the stock into the area that is left between the lid and the pan.
5. Just two hours of cooking at the lowest possible setting
6. Salmon should have a flaky texture and a temperature of $1/45$ degrees.
7. Prepare the fish with a generous amount of spinach.

66. Tuna with Zoodles Casserole

What we need:

- 1 liter of almond milk that has not been sweetened
- 1 cup ragged mozzarella
- Four medium-sized zucchinis
- Three cans of tuna fish in brine
- 1 cup ragged cheddar cheese
- Grass-fed butter, softened to the extent of four teaspoons
- As required, pepper-salt may be used.

Cooking method:

1. To begin, cut your zucchini into long, thin strips using a julienne peeler to create the appearance of noodles.
2. In a bowl, combine melted butter, shredded cheese, milk, and tuna.
3. Sprinkle pepper-salt over top in copious amounts.
4. Spray your slow cooker with a product that contains coconut oil to grease it.
5. Start by adding partly of the Zoodles, and finally do again the process with the remaining sauce.
6. After you have used up all of the ingredients, sprinkle some mozzarella cheese on top.
7. Within close proximity to the lid of the pan.

8. Cook for only 30 minutes.
9. Please serve it hot!

67. Broccoli and Mahi-Mahi Platter

What we need:

- 16 ounces of the product, either fresh or thawed mahi-mahi
- ½ ounces of broccoli that is still fresh
- A little amount of dried red pepper flakes
- Two teaspoons of broth made from vegetables
- Olive oil to the amount of ½ teaspoons
- ½ tablespoons of ginger that have been crushed
- ½ teaspoons worth of garlic paste
- As required, pepper-salt may be used.
- A few drops of lemon juice

Cooking method:

1. Olive oil should be used to coat the fish completely, and the fish should be seasoned on both sides.
2. Place the broccoli florets in the slow cooker.
3. After adding the fish, position it so that it is next to the lid of the pan.
4. Slow cooking for two to three hours at a low temperature. At its thickest portion, the fish should have a temperature of 145 degrees.
5. When the time is up, give it a taste, and then sprinkle some salt over it.
6. Place the fish and vegetables in a bowl, and then drizzle some lemon juice over the top before serving.

68. Surf and Turf

What we need:

- 2 (3-ounce) filet mignons Fine salt from the seaside and freshly ground black pepper
- Shell-on, buttery, and deveined prawns or large shrimp, of two different varieties with the shells on
- 2 tablespoons of the ketogenic cook's preferred fat, for fricasseeing
- 1 cup of Easy Basil Hollandaise to be used for serving

Cooking method:

1. The fillets should be seasoned well with pepper-salt on both sides. Let it sit at a comfortable level for 15 minutes once it has been allowed to reach that temperature.
2. Bring a frying pan up to a temperature of medium-high. When seasoning the shrimp, pepper and salt, especially pepper, should be used in large amounts.
3. In a heated pan, liquefy the fat, and when you're ready to cook the filets, bring them into the pan and fry them on both sides until they reach the level of doneness that you choose.
4. The fillets should be taken out of the cooker and left to chill for ten minutes. While the filets are resting, sauté the prawns in a pan of the same size until the shells have turned pink and the flesh is cooked through and no longer transparent. This should take around three minutes per side.
5. Put one steak on each individual plate. Add a prawn to the top of each dish, and then drizzle 2 tablespoons of the hollandaise sauce over the top. This meal tastes best when served right away.

69. Pork Chops

What we need:

- Bread crumbs (½ cup)
- (3-ounce) pork top-loin chops
- Olive oil (1 tablespoon)
- Herb Pesto (8 teaspoons)

Cooking method:

1. Set the microwave and prepare a microwave sheet by lining it with parchment or foil.
2. Place the bread crumbs in a shallow dish and spread them out evenly.

3. Coat each pork chop in bread crumbs, turning to ensure a uniform coating on both sides. Remove any extra crumbs by shaking.

4. In a large pan that is heated, bring the olive oil to the desired temperature.

5. The breaded pork chops need to be cooked for about three to four minutes on both sides so that they have a color that is similar to a golden brown.

6. Arrange the pork chops in a layer on a parchment sheet, and complete the cooking process in the microwave.

7. Cover the top of each pork chop with two teaspoons' worth of the herb pesto and set aside.

8. Place the chops in a microwave that has been prepared and bake for about 12 to 15 minutes.

9. The pork chops are done when they are removed from the microwave and allowed to relax for a few minutes before being served.

10. Warm the herb pesto pork chops and serve them with roasted vegetables, mashed potatoes, or a fresh salad, as desired.

70. Risotto with Seafood

What we need:
- 1 medium-sized head of cauliflower, which has been removed from the center and separated into florets
- 2 tablespoons of ghee, butter, or coconut oil that has not been salted
- 2 tablespoons of onion pieces, diced
- 1 small clove of garlic, chopped very coarsely
- ½ cups of mascarpone or cream cheese, each weighing 4 ounces
- Fine salt from the seaside and grated black pepper
- ½ cups of chicken broth
- ¼.0 ounces of grated Parmesan and cheddar
- 2 cups of crab meat, cooked shrimp, or pieces of langoustine that have been cooked

Cooking method:
1. To prepare the "rice," put the cauliflower florets in a blender and chop them once they are the size of rice. This should take about 5 minutes. This should take about five minutes. Place it in a safe and sound place.

2. The ghee has to be heated in a cooker over a medium flame. After the oil has achieved the appropriate temperature, the garlic and onions should be added. While they are sautéing for two minutes, the mixture of the onions and garlic should be stirred often.

3. Add the cauliflower rice as well as the mascarpone, and then season it with two or three pinches each of pepper-salt. Cooking the mixture while whisking it until the mascarpone is soft should take about a minute.

4. While whisking, gently incorporate the soup into the mixture. Cook it for four minutes, or until the "rice" has reached the desired degree of tenderness.

5. Include the Parmesan cheese and the cooked shrimp, and stir to combine; simmer for a second or two to warm everything through; then season to taste with pepper-salt, if necessary, and serve.

6. You may keep supplementary products in the cooler for up to three days if you place them in a container that can be sealed. It should be warmed thoroughly in a pan that has been lightly greased and set over medium heat.

71. Tilapia with Chili-Garlic-Butter

What we need:

- Four fillets of tilapia, either freshly prepared or thawed from frozen
- Two teaspoons of butter made from grass-fed animals
- Two cloves of garlic that have been minced
- ½ tablespoons of dried parsley
- ½ teaspoons of dried flakes of red chili pepper
- Pepper-salt only, as required.

Cooking method:

1. About 30 minutes before beginning the cooking process, soften the butter in the microwave for a few minutes.
2. Add minced garlic and dry parsley to the mixture.
3. To make it harder, chill it in the fridge.
4. After it has cooled and become firm enough to cut into patties, you are ready to begin preparing supper.
5. Take a piece of aluminum foil and arrange it so that it is flat.
6. Place one fillet in the center of the dish.
7. Repeat the process so that each of the four fillets has its own sheet.
8. Sprinkle a generous amount of pepper-salt over them.

9. Each filet should have a big dollop of butter on it.
10. Seal the edges of the foil after wrapping it securely around the item.
11. Place it in the slow cooker, and set the timer for two hours.
12. The fish should be flaky and cooked to ¹⁄45 degrees.
13. Include a side of vegetables with your meal!

72. Asian-Inspired Tilapia

What we need:
- Four fillets of tilapia, either freshly prepared or thawed from frozen
- Carrots cut in eighths, eight medium-sized ones
- Three cloves of garlic that have been minced
- ½ tablespoons of butter from grass-fed cows
- One and a half milligrams of ground ginger
- Turmeric ground to the equivalent of ½ tablespoons
- A splash of lime juice
- Salt to taste

Cooking method:
1. For each fillet, cut a square of aluminum foil.
2. Place two carrots on each piece of foil.
3. Carrots and fish may both benefit from being seasoned with ginger, turmeric, and a little bit of salt.
4. Evenly distribute the garlic cloves across the surface.
5. After slathering some butter on the top of the fillets, make sure the foil is well sealed.
6. Place the packages into the slow cooker; it's alright if they have to be stacked.
7. Cook for two hours on high heat.
8. Add a few drops of lime juice before serving.

73. Simple Salmon with Lemon

What we need:

- One and a half ounces of a dry white wine
- 2 kilograms of skin-on salmon, either fresh or thawed from frozen
- ½ teaspoon dried dill
- Two glasses full of water
- One lemon, cut into slices
- One shallot, cut into slices
- ½ teaspoon dried parsley
- As required, pepper-salt may be used.
- ½ teaspoons worth of garlic paste
- When it comes to cooking, olive oil is essential.

Cooking method:

1. Put the water, wine, lemon, shallot, and dry spice in a slow cooker.
2. The cooking process takes around a quarter of an hour.
3. Season the salmon with black pepper and salt, and then arrange it on a platter with the skin side facing down.
4. Cook for forty-five minutes before checking the dish. If it hasn't finished cooking yet, give it another 15 minutes of time in the microwave.
5. When the flakes have formed, sprinkle with olive oil and serve!

74. Flank Steak with Horseradish and Garlic

What we need:

- Horseradish, arranged to make 2 tablespoons
- Olive oil, one tablespoon's worth
- Salt, ½.5 teaspoons
- 4 minced garlic cloves
- Flank steak, one-pound cut of food splash

Cooking method:

1. Turn the broiler to medium heat.

2. Gather the first four ingredients in a bowl and mix them together. Coat both sides of the steak with the concoction.

3. Spray cooking spray on a rack for a grill pan and place the steak on top of it. Broil over high heat for four to five minutes per side, or until desired doneness is reached.

4. Take away from heat, broil, and then wait 5 minutes before serving. Steak should be sliced thinly against the grain, across the thickness.

75. Asian Chicken Satay

What we need:
- 2 lime juice
- Chicken breast (12 ounces)
- Brown sugar (2 tablespoons)
- Cumin
- Minced garlic (1 tablespoon)

Cooking method:
1. Mix the lime juice, brown sugar, pepper, salt, cumin, and garlic together in a bowl. Mix elements to make a marinade.
2. To the marinade, add the chicken breast strips, turning to coat each piece well.
3. Marinating the chicken for at least 30 minutes, or overnight, will let the flavors develop to their full potential.
4. Prepare a grill or grill pan by heating it over medium heat.
5. Marinated chicken pieces are threaded onto skewers with enough room between them.
6. Prepare the chicken skewers by grilling them for three to four minutes both side until they are no longer pink in the middle and have developed a nice sear. If you want to avoid sticking or shattering them, be careful while turning them.
7. Any residual marinade may be used to baste the chicken as it grills for an added dose of flavor and moisture.
8. After the skewers have finished cooking, remove them from the grill and put the chicken aside to relax for a few moments.
9. When eaten with peanut sauce or any dipping sauce of your choice, the Asian Chicken Satay is a versatile dish that works well both as an appetizer and as a main course.
10. Serve the satay with steamed rice and a side salad for a filling supper.

11. Asian Chicken Satay, marinated in lime juice and flavored with fragrant spices, is delicate and tasty.

76. Beef Stir-up

What we need:
- Lean ground beef (½ pound)
- Shredded cabbage (½ cup)
- Herb Pesto (¼ cup)
- 6 hamburger buns
- Sweet onion (½ cup)

Cooking method:
1. Put oil in a big pan and warm it over medium heat.
2. Slice a sweet onion and sauté it in the pan until it becomes transparent and caramelized.
3. The onions should be moved to one side of the pan, and the ground beef should be added to the other.
4. To ensure the ground beef is well cooked, brown it in a skillet while breaking it up with a spoon.
5. Shredded cabbage should be added to the pan with the ground meat and onions. Add two to three more minutes of cooking time to get a tiny wilt out of the cabbage.
6. Put the heat on low and stir in the herb pesto. The pesto should be well mixed into the steak and cabbage.
7. Let it simmer for a few more minutes so the flavors can combine.
8. As the beef mixture cooks, toast the buns in the microwave until they are golden brown and crunchy.
9. Turn off the heat after the meat combination has reached the desired doneness for you.
10. To assemble the beef stir-up, spread the bottom halves of the toasted hamburger buns with mayonnaise and then heap a heaping spoonful of the beef and cabbage mixture on top.
11. To finish the sandwiches, place the top halves of the buns on top of the beef mixture.
12. Beef stir-up is ready to be served as a savory and filling supper right away.

SNACKS

77. Crust-Free Pizza

What we need:

- 1 pound of pork that has been ground up
- Pizza with two teaspoons of seasoning,
- 1 tomato preserve can
- 2 cups of mozzarella
- 1 pound of beef that has been ground up
- 1 fluid ounce of peppers
- 1 ounce (or one cup) of black olives
- 1 jar of pizza sauce
- 1 measure of onions
- 30 individual pepperoni slices
- 1 ounce (or cup) of mushroom

Cooking method:

1. Take a pan, lightly brown both of the pork pieces. They should be placed in the slow cooker.
2. Include some fresh herbs and vegetables in this. At this point, you should start pouring in the sauce and the tomatoes.
3. Distribute the cheese in an equal layer. Include some pepperoni. Prepare over low heat for a total of three hours. Put all of the crust's components through the food processor.
4. They should be arranged such that they cover the base of the stove. Mix together all of the components that will make up the filling.
5. Transfer the mixture to the slow cooker and set it on the lowest setting. Over a heat setting that is low, prepare for a total of three hours.
6. Wait a half an hour for it to cool down.

78. Cilantro-lime Flounder

What we need:

- Mayonnaise (¼ cup)
- Ground black pepper
- One pressed lime juice
- Cilantro, chopped (½ cup)
- One lime zest
- (3-ounce) flounder fillets

Cooking method:

1. Put the microwave on at a temperature of 400 degrees Fahrenheit.
2. Mayonnaise, lime juice, lime zest, and cilantro should be mixed together in a small bowl and stirred until the ingredients are completely incorporated.
3. Place all four pieces of foil on a surface that has been well sanitized before doing so.
4. In the middle of each square, position one fillet of flounder.
5. After allowing some time to pass, proceed to apply mayonnaise all over the fillets.
6. Pepper is the perfect condiment to use for seasoning them.
7. To get the fish ready for baking, make a package out of the aluminum foil, wrap it around the fish, and then place it on a baking sheet.
8. They should be baked for around 5 minutes.
9. Serve the meal after first removing it from its package.

79. Mashed Parmesan and Cauliflower Gravy

What we need:

- 5 cups of cauliflower florets that have been chopped
- Five cloves of garlic that have been minced
- A total of four tablespoons of full-fat cream
- Four teaspoons of butter made from grass-fed animals
- ½ teaspoon dried rosemary
- Parmesan cheese is equivalent to three teaspoons.
- Pepper-salt
- A sufficient amount of boiling water to cover the cauliflower
- The equivalent of two cups of chicken stock

- Twelve glasses' worth of cream
- ½ teaspoons of thyme, dried

Cooking method:

1. The florets of cauliflower should be placed in the slow cooker. Sprinkle over a sufficient amount of boiling water to cover it.
2. Right next to the pan's cover. It was cooked at a high temperature for a period of four hours. Cauliflower has to be cooked until it is extremely soft.
3. In a separate pan, start melting the butter about five minutes before the cauliflower is done cooking.
4. To get a golden color, combine the garlic with the mixture.
5. At the same time, combine all of the ingredients for the in a separate pan.
6. After bringing things to cook, let it steam for fifteen minutes.
7. After the cauliflower has finished cooking, swirl in the garlic, and then add the cream, cheese, and spices. To get a smooth consistency similar to that of mashed potatoes, puree the ingredients using either an engaged mixer or a standard mixer in stages.
8. To finish off the gravy, combine and season as desired with salt, pepper, and other spices.
9. Present the mashed potatoes with the gravy on the side.

80. Meatballs

What we need:

- A total of four cups of beef stock
- 4 kg of beef that was raised on grass
- Cumin to the tune of two tablespoons
- The equivalent of four tablespoons of sugar-free tomato paste
- Paprika, to taste, two tablespoons
- Seasoning with two tablespoons of Italian oregano
- As required, pepper-salt may be used.

Cooking method:

1. Mix the meat with the spices, and then roll the mixture into balls.
2. Place it in the slow cooker you have.
3. Combine the stock and tomato paste in a blender until it is completely smooth.
4. Move the meatballs to the pan where they will cook.

5. Within close proximity to the lid of the pan.
6. Putting it in the microwave at a high temperature for a period of two hours
7. Please serve it hot!

81. Sweet and Spicy Shrimp

What we need:
- 2 kg of raw prawns, which have been de-wrapped and washed
- 3/4 cup olive oil
- A little amount of dried red pepper flakes
- Stevia in liquid form, four tablespoons' worth
- One teaspoon of sweet paprika
- Sriracha to taste, two tablespoons
- As required, pepper-salt may be used.

Cooking method:
1. Mix olive oil, stevia, Sriracha, paprika, red pepper flakes, pepper, and salt in a pan.
2. Within close proximity to the lid of the pan.
3. Putting it through the microwave at a high temperature for half an hour.
4. Taste the sauce and adjust the amount of sweetness and spice to suit your preferences.
5. After adding the raw shrimp, whisk the mixture to coat it.
6. Within close proximity to the lid of the pan.
7. Putting it through a high-temperature cooking process for ten minutes.
8. Serve!

82. Zucchini and Beef-Stuffed Peppers

What we need:

- Four poblano peppers
- 1 ½ cups chopped zucchinis
- Seven tablespoons of tomato sauce with no added sugar
- A pound and a half of ground beef
- Onion, chopped, to the extent of five teaspoons
- A little less than a tablespoon of shredded mozzarella cheese
- As required, pepper-salt may be used.
- Water

Cooking method:

1. To prepare the poblano peppers for cooking, remove the seeds and cut them in half lengthwise.
2. Cook the onions and ground beef together in a pan until they are browned.
3. Cook for about a minute to let the flavors meld together after mixing in the zucchini and the sauce.
4. Put the filling in the peppers.
5. Put approximately an inch's worth of water into your slow cooker, and then add a few teaspoons of water.
6. Add the peppers to the dish.
7. Cook for three and a half hours on high. The beef must be cooked to an internal temperature of 160 degrees.
8. When the allotted time has passed, sprinkle cheese over the top.
9. To melt the cheese, place the sandwich under a hot broiler for only three minutes.
10. Serve!

83. Cheesy Spaghetti Squash

What we need:

- One large spaghetti squash, which weighs about 5 pounds
- 3/4 cup shredded mozzarella
- Cottage cheese equaling 5 ounces
- ¼ cup of parsley that has been chopped
- ¼ cups of butter from grass-fed cows
- 1 ounce and 5 ounces of grated Parmesan cheese
- Two cloves of garlic that have been minced
- Pepper-salt

Cooking method:

1. Cut your squash in half lengthwise, cutting it part by part.
2. Place it in the slow cooker with the cut side facing down, right next to the lid of the pan.
3. Prepare it by cooking it at a high temperature for two to three hours.
4. When the allotted time has passed, carefully remove the squash.
5. Put the butter and garlic in the pan so that they may melt.
6. Remove the seeds from the cooked squash while protecting your hands with microwave mitts.
7. Use a fork to separate the meat from the bones, and then return to the kitchen.
8. Combine the cottage cheese with the parmesan cheese in a mixing bowl.
9. Add a little pepper-salt to taste.
10. After that, give it a thorough whisk.
11. Mozzarella should be sprinkled on top, and then the dish should be moved close to the lid of the slow cooker so that any additional heat may melt the cheese.
12. Add some chopped parsley on top, and then dig in!

84. Fresh Veggies with Herbs

What we need:

- 2 and a half cups of sliced zucchini
- Two coffee glasses filled with yellow bell peppers
- A couple of cups of crisp spinach
- 1/½ cup sweet onion
- One and a half cups of grape tomatoes
- There are ½ cups of olive oil.
- ½ espresso cups worth of balsamic vinegar
- Two teaspoons of freshly chopped basil
- One tablespoon of fresh thyme that has been chopped

Cooking method:

1. Mix the veggies together in big dish.
2. Blend the balsamic vinegar and olive oil together in a separate container to make an emulsion.
3. 3: Mix the herbs into the basin containing the dressing.
4. Place the vegetables inside the slow cooker.
5. Pour the dressing on top of the salad and toss it up, then place the lid on the pan.
6. It should be cooked at a low temperature for three hours, with stirring taking place every hour.
7. Serve!

85. Prosciutto-Garlic Green Beans

What we need:

- 5 kg of freshly picked green beans
- 4-ounces prosciutto
- Ten cloves of garlic that have been minced
- A third of a cup of brown sugar
- As much water as is required to cover the beans
- ½ cups of butter from grass-fed cows

- To enhance the flavor, pepper-salt were added.

Cooking method:

1. Throw everything into the pot or the cooker.
2. After cooking it at a high temperature for one hour, reduce it to a low temperature for four hours.
3. After that, give it a taste and season it with more pepper-salt if you feel it needs it.

86. Pizza Casserole

What we need:

- 2 boneless chicken breasts in the package
- 2 whole cloves of garlic
- 1 level teaspoon of spice, a dash of Italian pepper
- Eight fluid ounces of tomato paste
- 1 piece of fresh mozzarella half a cup 1 bay leaf, 0.25 tablespoons of salt

Cooking method:

1. Position the chicken breasts into the cooker on low.
2. Combine in the other ingredients, except the cheese.
3. Prepare over a low heat for a total of four hours.
4. Once the meal is complete, finish it off by sprinkling some cheese on top.

87. Veggie Burger

What we need:

- Veggie burger patties, either store-bought or homemade
- Burger buns
- Red onion, minced
- Avocado scored
- Pickles
- Tomato
- Lettuce leaves
- Condiments of choice, such as ketchup, mustard, or vegan mayo, to enhance the flavors according to a unique taste

Cooking method:

1. Bring a grill that fits on a burner to a medium heat.
2. Heat and grill the vegetable burger patties according to package Cooking method or your preferred way.
3. While the vegetable burgers cook, gently toast the buns to a golden brown and crisp texture.
4. Top the toasted buns with avocado, tomato, red onion, lettuce, and pickles after cooking the vegetarian patties.
5. Spread ketchup, mustard, or vegan mayo on buns for flavor and moisture.
6. Imagine the robust texture and taste of the cooked vegetable patties on top of the toppings.
7. Gently push the burgers into the top half of the buns.
8. Serve veggie burgers with sweet potato fries for a healthy supper.
9. Transfer and cool the sweet potato fries.
10. Enjoy the tasty blend of warm and veggie burgers.

88. Peppers Salsa

What we need:

- Red bell peppers (1 pound)
- One onion, chopped
- One jalapeño pepper, chopped
- Apple cider vinegar (½ cup)
- Two banana peppers, chopped
- Garlic, minced (two teaspoons)
- Three tablespoons of cilantro
- Granulated sugar
- One chopped green bell pepper

Cooking method:

1. Put the banana peppers, garlic, jalapeno peppers, red bell peppers, onion, green bell pepper, sugar, and apple cider vinegar onto a wide pan that has been previously prepared, and mix all of the ingredients together very well.

2. Get the water to a simmer while continuously stirring it during the process of bringing it to a boil.
3. After one more hour of cooking, reduce the temperature to a low setting and continue to simmer.
4. After some time has elapsed, the cilantro should be added, and the dish should be allowed to continue cook over a steam for around 15 minutes.
5. Take it out of the frying pan in its entirety.
6. Hold off for twenty minutes before you try to touch it again.
7. Put the salsa in a container that will keep the air out, and then store it in the refrigerator.
8. To serve, mix together all ingredients and refrigerate before serving with prepared tortilla chips.

89. Cheeseburger Casserole

What we need:

Cheese Sauce:

- A cup of butter
- Two teaspoons of arrowroot flour
- ½ teaspoon of pepper
- 1.5 cups milk
- A half teaspoon and a half of salt
- 2 cups cheddar

Casserole:

- 2 kg of beef that has been ground
- 0.5 cups of chopped onion
- Chili powder to the extent of two teaspoons
- A half-cup of ketchup that is sugar-free and does not contain any
- One teaspoon and one-fifth of tomato paste
- Olive oil to the amount of two teaspoons
- Two separate cloves of garlic
- 2.2 ounces of Dijon mustard 0.2 ounces of beef broth
- A quarter of a cup of relish (dill pickle)

Cooking method:

Casserole:

1. Cook the meat, garlic, and onion in order to get them ready for use.
2. Include any other constituents that may be required.
3. After giving the ingredients a good combining, put them to a moderate simmer.
4. Place the items in the saucepan that will be used for cooking.
5. Prepare over low heat for a total of three hours.

Cheese Sauce:

1. Combine the milk and arrowroot powder.
2. Begin by melting the butter.
3. Mix in the milk as you add it.
4. Add cheese.
5. Mix in the relish with a spoon.
6. Distribute it evenly over the dish's surface.
7. You may use tortillas or low-carb crackers in this recipe if you want it to have a little more of a crunch. To get an accurate calculation of the net carbohydrates, just keep the amount of the dish in mind.

90. Deep Dish Pizza Crust

What we need:

- 1 floret of cauliflower in its head
- 2 eggs
- Italian seasoning, one teaspoon's worth
- A half cup and a half of Italian cheese
- 0.25 grams of salt in a teaspoon

Cooking method:

1. Prepare the cauliflower by chopping it and processing it.
2. Combine the remaining components in the mixture.
3. Add the cauliflower and mix.
4. Put it in the slow cooker.
5. Put some pressure on it to create a shell.

6. Prepare on a high heat for two hours.

91. Nachos

What we need:
- Low-carb tortilla chips
- An individual red onion
- Tinned tomatoes weighing in at 500 grams
- One teaspoon and one-fifth of tomato paste
- 500 grams of beef were crushed into a powder.
- A half of a teaspoon's worth of chili powder
- You are free to pick the toppings that go on your burger in accordance with your tastes.

Cooking method:
1. Sear the meat in the pan until it is browned.
2. Put the paste and tomatoes in a mixer and combine awaiting soft.
3. Give it a vigorous stir.
4. Transfer the liquid to the inside of the cooker.
5. Include any additional ingredients or ingredients that are required.
6. Prepare over low heat for a period of two hours.
7. Pour the dip over the tortilla chips.
8. Add as many toppings as you'd like on your pizza.

92. Chicken Stir-Fry

What we need:
- Chicken breast (½ oz)
- Honey
- Vinegar (3 tbsp)
- Oil (2 tablespoon)
- Cooked hot rice
- Soy sauce
- Pineapple juice (3 tbsp)
- Mixed vegetables (3 cups)

Cooking method:

1. After you've washed the chicken and chopped it up, set it aside.
2. Take a cooker; mix the vinegar, soy sauce, pineapple juice, honey, and cornstarch in it. Give it a good stir, and then set it aside.
3. Once the pan is hot, put oil to it and then sauté the veggies for around three minutes after that, or until they are cooked but still have some crunch.
4. Remove them from the pan and discard them.
5. About four minutes should be spent cooking the chicken in the pan that has been heated.
6. Place the sauce in the dish, and stir it often until it becomes thick and bubbly.
7. Once again, add the veggies and give everything a good toss.
8. Continue to cook for one further minute.
9. To be served with the rice.

93. Cilantro-lime Flounder

What we need:

- Mayonnaise (¼ cup)
- Ground black pepper
- One pressed lime juice
- Cilantro, chopped (½ cup)
- One lime zest
- (3-ounce) flounder fillets

Cooking method:

1. Put the microwave on at a temperature of 400 degrees Fahrenheit.
2. Mayonnaise, lime juice, lime zest, and cilantro should be mixed together in a small bowl and stirred until the ingredients are completely incorporated.
3. Place all four pieces of foil on a surface that has been well sanitized before doing so.
4. In the middle of each square, position one fillet of flounder.
5. After allowing some time to pass, proceed to apply mayonnaise all over the fillets.
6. Pepper is the perfect condiment to use for seasoning them.
7. To get the fish ready for baking, make a package out of the aluminum foil, wrap it around the fish, and then place it on a baking sheet.

8. They should be baked for around 5 minutes.
9. Serve the meal after first removing it from its package.

94. Jalapeño Poppers

What we need:

- 10 fresh jalapeños, halved and seeded
- 8 oz. cream cheese, softened
- 1 cup grated cheddar cheese
- 10 slices of bacon, cooked and crushed
- 1 teaspoon garlic paste
- Salt and pepper to taste

Cooking Method:

1. Preheat the microwave.
2. Put the shredded cheddar, cream cheese, grind bacon, garlic paste, pepper, and salt into a bowl and mix them together until they are completely incorporated.
3. Put the mixture into the halves of the jalapeño peppers.
4. Once they have been placed on a microwave rack, bake them for fifteen to twenty minutes, or until the tops have a golden hue.
5. Serve while still heated.

95. Zucchini Chips

What we need:

- 2 medium zucchinis, lightly sliced
- 2 tablespoons of olive oil
- ¼ cup grated Parmesan cheese
- 1 teaspoon dried oregano
- Salt and pepper to taste

Cooking method:

1. At first preheat the microwave.
2. Tossing the zucchini slices in olive oil will ensure that they are evenly covered with the oil.

3. A basin should be used to blend the following what we need: Parmesan cheese, dried oregano, salt, and pepper.
4. To ensure that the zucchini slices are evenly coated, apply the Parmesan mixture to them.
5. Once the zucchini has been prepared, it should be placed on a baking pan.
6. The chips should be baked for two to three hours in order to get a crispier texture.
7. Before you serve it, you should wait until it has cooled down.

96. Buffalo Cauliflower Bites

What we need:
- 1 medium cauliflower, cut into florets
- ½ cup almond flour
- 2 teaspoon crushed garlic
- 1 teaspoon of onion paste
- ½ teaspoon paprika
- ¼ cup melted butter
- ¼ cup hot sauce (sugar-free)
- Ranch dressing for dipping

Cooking Method:
1. Preheat the microwave.
2. Combine garlic paste, smoked paprika, onion powder, and almond flour in a dish. Additionally, add garlic powder.
3. Cauliflower florets should be tossed in the mixture until they are completely covered.
4. Place the cauliflower so that it is arranged in one layer on a parchment-covered disc.
5. Put in the microwave and roast for fifteen to twenty-five minutes, so that the texture of the top is brown and crisp.
6. In a separate dish, combine the butter that has been melted with the spicy sauce.
7. Combine the buffalo sauce with the cauliflower that has been roasted.
8. Ranch dressing should be served alongside it for dipping.

Soup

97. Chicken Soup with Noodle

What we need:

- Chicken stew (1 ½ cups)
- Salt
- Cooked chicken (1 cup)
- Water
- Black pepper
- Carrot (¼ cup)
- Poultry seasoning (¼ tsp)
- Uncooked egg noodles (2 oz.)

Cooking method:

7. Place the water as well as the broth inside the slow cooker, and then adjust the temperature so that it is as low as it can go.
8. Salt, black pepper, and poultry spice are not already included in them; thus, these three spices will need to be added to them before they can be used.
9. The preparation of the chicken requires a number of steps, two of which are the cutting of the carrot and the paring of the bird.
10. They should be put into the broth at the same time as the noodles if you want the best results.
11. Approximately twenty-five minutes should be set aside in order to carry out the cooking operation.
12. Keep the temperature at a gentle simmer for around five minutes.

98. Chicken Vegetable soup

What we need:

- Unsalted butter
- Ground black pepper
- ½ diced sweet onion
- Chicken stock, one cup
- Thyme, chopped (one teaspoon)
- Two celery stalks, chopped
- Water
- Minced garlic (2 teaspoons)
- Cooked chicken breast, chopped (2 cups)
- One carrot, diced
- Parsley (two tablespoons)

Cooking method:

1. You may melt the butter in the pan you have by choosing a heat setting that is somewhere in the middle.
2. After adding the garlic and onion, continue to cook for approximately three more minutes.
3. After a certain amount of time has passed, you will want to add carrots, water, celery, and chicken stock to the pot.
4. The soup has to be brought to a simmer at this point.
5. Decrease the temperature to a low setting and keep going to steam at a low simmer for around thirty minutes.
6. After that, the thyme should be added, and the soup should be allowed to boil for an additional two minutes.
7. Pepper is the perfect condiment to use for seasoning them.
8. Before serving, garnish with chopped, fresh parsley.

99. Curried cauliflower soup

What we need:

- 3 cups of water
- One small cauliflower
- Unsalted butter (one teaspoon)
- One onion, chopped
- Sour cream (½ cup)
- Curry powder (two teaspoons)
- Garlic, minced (2 teaspoons)
- Cilantro, chopped (three tablespoons)

Cooking method:

1. Utilizing a big pan and heating it over a moderate setting will ensure that the butter is thoroughly melted.
2. Cooking the garlic and onion for around three minutes should be sufficient time.
3. Combine the cauliflower, water, and curry powder in a big dish.
4. After bringing the mixture to a rolling boil, lower the heat to a gentle simmer and go on cooking.
5. Maintain a low simmer for around twenty minutes.
6. Put the components in a grinder and prepare them so the mixture is a silky fluid.
7. Repeat the process of transferring the soup to the saucepan.
8. Mix in the finely chopped coriander as well as the sour cream.

100. Rice and Beef Soup

What we need:

- Extra-lean ground beef (½ pound)
- Beef broth, prepared (1 cup)
- Black pepper
- One sweet onion, chopped
- Thyme, chopped (1 teaspoon)
- Minced garlic

- White rice, uncooked (½ cup)
- ½ cup green beans
- One celery stalk, chopped
- Water

Cooking method:

1. Put the pan on a low temperature and add the minced meat. The meat needs to be cooked for a certain amount of time until it turns brown.
2. Reduce the amount of excess fat.
3. After some time has passed, the onion and garlic should be added to the pan. You should cook them for around three minutes.
4. After that, add the rice, celery, beef stew, and water. Get the water to cook, and then continue to steam. Keep the temperature at a low simmer for about a half an hour.
5. After that, toss in the thyme and the legumes, and then maintain the pot on a low heat for approximately three more minutes.
6. Remove them from the burning environment.
7. Pepper should be used to season them.

101. Cauliflower and Bacon Soup

What we need:

- 6 slices bacon, chopped
- 1 medium head cauliflower, chopped into florets
- 2 cloves garlic, minced
- 1 small onion, finely chopped
- 1 cup cream
- 4 cups chicken stew
- minced onions for garnish
- Salt-black pepper to taste
- 1 cup grated cheese

Cooking method:

1. Preparing some bacon by chopping it. In a large saucepan set over a heat source of medium, cook it until it is lovely and crispy. Take away the bacon and set it sideways, but do not throw away the fat in the pan.
2. To soften the onion and garlic, cook them in the bacon grease in the same saucepan.

3. Then, after another 3–5 minutes of sautéing, throw in some cauliflower florets.

4. At this point, the chicken stock should be added to the dish, and it should be heated to a cook.

5. Lower the heat and give the cauliflower a few more minutes of boiling.

6. An immersion blender may be used to mix the soup nicely. Without an immersion blender, purée the soup in batches by a conventional mixer.

7. To make a soup creamier, add some heavy cream and grated cheddar cheeses, then cook the mixture so that the cheese is completely melt.

8. Spice with black pepper and salt to taste.

9. The cauliflower and bacon chowder is hot, bubbling, and topped with crispy bacon and chopped green onions.

102. Thermion of Shrimp

What we need:
- A total of ¼ more cups of softened ghee or unsalted spread are to be added at the very end if using pig skins, for a total of ½ cups of fat if using margarine.
- 2 cups of chopped fresh shiitake
- ¼ cups of chopped onions
- Large shrimp (about 30 per pound), peeled and deveined
- Chicken bone stock, homemade or store-bought; enough to fill a cup
- 1 package of aged cream cheese (about 8 ounces)
- 3/4 smashed cup of cheddar
- Pork skins, smashed and divided into ½ cups (optional)
- ½ cups of Parmesan cheddar cheese ground

Cooking method:
1. Turn the grill up to high heat.

2. Over moderate heat, melt ½ cup of ghee in a cast-iron pan until it is liquid. In batches, stir fry the mushrooms and onions for about 5 minutes or until they have a deep, rich color.

3. Mix in the shrimp, and then carry on cooking for another three minutes so the shrimp are opaque all the way through.

4. The next step is to pulse the cream cheese and mushroom soup in a grinder until it's mushy, then add it to the skillet.

5. Blend in the cheddar and 1 cup of the crushed pork skins. Pour the mixture into a goulash dish.
6. Parmesan cheese and the remaining ½ cups of smashed pig skins (if used) should be spread over the goulash's peak. If you're using pig skins, pour ¼ cup of melted ghee on top.
7. Warm the cheddar for 2–4 minutes in the microwave, or until it reaches the desired texture, before grilling.
8. You may keep extra things cold for up to four days in the refrigerator's sealed section.
9. Warm in a dish that has been heated on the stove for 4 minutes, or until the food is fully cooked.

103. Broccoli and Cheddar Soup

What we need:
- 2 cups grated cheese
- 2 cups of broccoli florets
- ¼ cup unsalted butter
- ¼ cup almond flour
- 4 cups of chicken stew
- Pepper-Salt to taste

Cooking Method:
1. Put broccoli in a saucepan and cook it until it is soft.
2. Almond flour must be stirred into the melted butter in a separate cooker to create a roux.
3. Using a whisk, gradually incorporate the broth until it is completely smooth.
4. Incorporate heavy cream, cheddar cheese, and broccoli that have been cooked.
5. The cheese should be dissolved, and the soup should be cooked all the way through before serving.
6. For seasoning, use salt and pepper.

104. Chicken and Vegetable Soup

What we need:

- 1 cup chopped celery
- Salt-pepper to taste
- 4 cups of chicken stew
- 2 cups shredded cooked chicken
- 1 cup sliced carrots
- 1 cup of cauliflower rice
- ½ cup diced onion
- 2 minced garlic cloves
- Fresh basil for garnish

Cooking Method:

1. Onions, garlic, carrots, and celery should be sautéed in a saucepan until they become tenderer.
2. Incorporate dried thyme, minced chicken, rice made from cauliflower, and chicken stew into the mixture.
3. Allow the veggies to simmer until they are soft.
4. For seasoning, use salt and pepper.
5. Immediately before serving, garnish with fresh parsley.

105. Creamy Tomato Basil Soup

What we need:

- 1 cup heavy cream
- 2 cans (28oz each) of crushed tomatoes
- Salt and pepper to taste
- Fresh basil for garnish
- ¼ cup unsalted butter
- 2 cloves garlic, minced
- ¼ cup grated Parmesan cheese
- 1 teaspoon dried basil

Cooking Method:

1. Melt the butter in a cooker and fry the minced garlic awaiting it becomes aromatic.
2. Mix the smashed tomatoes, and then reduce the heat to a simmer.
3. Heavy cream, grated Parmesan cheese and dried basil should be stirred in.
4. Reduce heat to low and simmer, stirring periodically, for 15–20 minutes.
5. For seasoning, use salt and pepper.
6. Toss in some fresh basil just before serving for a garnish.

106. Keto Spicy Cauliflower Soup

What we need:

- 1 head cauliflower, chopped
- 1 onion, diced
- 3 cloves garlic, minced
- 4 cups vegetable stew
- 1 cup almond milk
- 1 teaspoon curry powder
- 1/2 teaspoon cayenne pepper
- Black pepper and Salt to taste
- Fresh cilantro for garnish

Cooking Method:

1. Cook the onions and garlic in a saucepan until they become more pliable.
2. Cauliflower, vegetable broth, almond milk, curry powder, and cayenne pepper should be added to the ingredients.
3. The cauliflower should be cooked until it is soft, so bring it to cook, then decrease the heat and simmer.
4. In order to get a smooth consistency, use an immersion blender.
5. For seasoning, use salt and pepper.
6. Before serving, garnish with fresh cilantro.

107. Seafood Chowder

What we need:

- 1 cup heavy cream
- 2 cloves garlic, minced
- ¼ cup onion, diced
- 1 lb mixed seafood (shrimp, scallops, fish), chopped
- 1 cup cauliflower, diced
- Salt to taste
- ½ cup chopped celery
- 2 tablespoons unsalted butter
- 4 cups vegetable or fish stew
- Black pepper to taste

Cooking Method:

1. It is recommended that the garlic, onions, and celery be cooked in butter in a pot until they reach the desired level of tenderness.
2. Add some Old Bay seasoning to the mixture, along with some cauliflower, fish, stock, and heavy cream. Mix well.
3. Maintaining a low simmer for the combination will ensure that the seafood is completely cooked and that the cauliflower is tender.
4. When seasoning food, use both salt and pepper.
5. To finish off the dish, sprinkle some fresh parsley on top just before serving.

108. Keto Cream of Asparagus Soup

What we need:

- 4 cups of chicken or vegetable stew
- 3 minced garlic cloves
- Lemon zest for garnish
- 1 cup heavy cream
- 2 tablespoons of olive oil
- 2 bunches of asparagus, trimmed and chopped
- 1 onion, diced

- Salt-pepper to taste

Cooking Method:
1. Onions and garlic should be cooked in olive oil in a saucepan until they become tenderer.
2. A few minutes after adding the asparagus, continue to sauté the vegetables.
3. To prepare the asparagus, pour in the stock and let it boil until it is soft.
4. In order to get a smooth consistency, use an immersion blender.
5. After adding the heavy cream and stirring, heat the mixture until it boils.
6. For seasoning, use salt and pepper.
7. Add some lemon zest as a garnish right before serving.

109. Mexican Chicken Avocado Lime Soup

What we need:
- Fresh cilantro for garnish
- 2 avocados, diced
- 2 cups shredded cooked chicken
- 4 cups of chicken stew
- 1 can (14 oz) diced tomatoes with green chilies
- 2 teaspoons of cumin
- ¼ cup of lime juice
- Salt and pepper to taste
- 1 teaspoon chili powder

Cooking Method:
1. Chicken, diced avocados, diced tomatoes, green chilies, chicken stew, lime juice, cumin, and chili powder should be mixed together in a saucepan.
2. Simmer for ten to fifteen minutes after bringing to a simmer.
3. For seasoning, use salt and pepper.
4. Before serving, garnish with fresh cilantro.

110. Roasted Red Pepper and Tomato Soup

What we need:
- 2 red bell peppers, roasted and chopped
- 2 tablespoons of olive oil
- 4 large tomatoes, roasted and skinned
- 1 onion, diced
- 3 minced garlic cloves
- 4 cups of chicken stew
- ½ cup cream
- 1 teaspoon paprika
- Salt and pepper to taste

Cooking Method:
1. When cooking onions and garlic in a cooker with olive oil, the garlic and onions should be cooked until they become softer.
2. Roasted tomatoes and red peppers should be added to the preparation.
3. Once the broth has been added, the mixture should be brought to a simmer.
4. Utilize an immersion blender to ensure that the mixture is entirely smooth before proceeding with the recipe.
5. Both the heavy cream and the smoked paprika need to be mixed into the mixture.
6. When seasoning food, use both salt and pepper.
7. Before the dish is served, fresh basil should be added as a garnish ingredient.

111. Thai Coconut Chicken Soup

What we need:
- 2 cups cooked chicken, shredded
- 1 can (14 oz) coconut milk
- 4 cups of chicken stew
- 1 red bell pepper, thinly sliced
- 1 zucchini cut into small cubed
- 2 tablespoons Thai red curry paste
- 2 tablespoons fish sauce

- 1 tablespoon lime juice
- Fresh cilantro for garnish

Cooking Method:

1. Chicken, coconut milk, chicken stew, sliced bell pepper, and spiralizer zucchini should be mixed together in a saucepan along with the chicken.
2. Start by bringing the mixture to a simmer, then toss in the fish sauce, lime juice, and Thai red curry paste.
3. Warm for fifteen to twenty minutes.
4. Before serving, garnish with fresh cilantro.

112. Egg Drop Soup

What we need:

- 4 cups of chicken stew
- 2 red onions, chopped
- 2 eggs
- Salt and white pepper to taste
- 1 teaspoon sesame oil

Cooking Method:

1. The chicken stock should be brought to a simmer in a saucepan.
2. With a gentle swirling motion, gradually add the beaten eggs to the broth that is boiling.
3. Stir in some chopped green onions.
4. Sesame oil should be drizzled on top.
5. White pepper and salt should be used to season.
6. Serve the dish warm.

113. Zucchini Soup

What we need:

- There should be 3 cups of vegetable stock.
- 2 kg of zucchini that has been chopped
- Two cloves of garlic that have been minced
- 1 and a half tablespoons of minced onion 14 tablespoons of basil leaves

- ½ milliliters of olive oil
- As required, pepper and salt may be used.

Getting ready:
1. Take a cooker, warm the olive oil across medium to low flame.
2. Stir fry the garlic and onion together for around five minutes in the heated cooker.
3. The remaining components should then be poured into your heater.
4. Within close proximity to the lid of the pan.
5. Preparing it over a period of two hours at a low temperature.
6. When the allotted time has passed, utilize a standard mixer to pulp the broth in stages.
7. Taste them and season them with more pepper and salt, if necessary.

114. Cobbler topped with Chicken Gravy

What we need:
- 2 tablespoons of ghee or unsalted butter (or, if dairy-free, coconut oil);
- 112 cups of mushrooms, sliced into pieces
- ¼ cup of onion pieces, diced
- 2 celery ribs, thinly sliced and sliced again
- 1 cup of asparagus that has been sliced
- 1 teaspoon of fine-grained salt from the ocean
- Ground dark pepper to the amount of 12 tablespoons
- 4 ounces of cream cheese for the 12 servings
- 34 cups of chicken bone juice, scones that were either made locally or purchased from a shop.
- 4 really large egg whites
- 1 cup of almond flour that has been whitened
- 1 teaspoon of the powder used for heating
- ¼ milligram of very fine ocean salt
- 3 tablespoons of frozen margarine (or lard, if dairy-free), cut into small pieces Thyme, fresh and for use in trimming
- Ghee that has been melted and used as a spread or for bathing

Getting ready:

1. Broil at 400 degrees. Medium-heated cast-iron pans soften ghee. Fry the mushrooms and onions until they're darker, and then stir the celery and asparagus for three more minutes.

2. Sprinkle black pepper and salt on sliced chicken breast on all sides. Brown and fry the chicken in a pan. It should be undercooked. Mix the cream cheese in the pan until there are no lumps. Enter the broth rapidly but cautiously. Start making scones for the fixing after storing it.

3. Start by whisking the egg whites in a mixing dish so that they're firm. Mix the powder, salt, and almond flour in a similar-sized container.

4. After that, mix in the spread. (The scones won't turn out if the spread isn't refrigerated.) Gently spread the flour mixture over the egg whites. Use a big spoon or frozen yogurt scooper to scoop out the dough and shape it into 2-inch scones. Maintain margarine clusters.

5. Mix the bread rolls with the mixture in the pan. Prepare for 12–15 minutes until the bread rolls are black enough. Add thyme and melted butter. Water- or airtight containers can store additional items in the icebox for three days. It should be cooked well in a dish.

115. Traditional Chicken-vegetable Soup

What we need:
- Unsalted butter
- Ground black pepper
- ½ diced sweet onion
- Chicken stock, one cup
- Thyme, chopped (one teaspoon)
- Two celery stalks, chopped
- Parsley (two tablespoons)
- One carrot, diced
- Minced garlic (2 teaspoons)
- 2 cups boiled chicken breast, chopped
- Water

Getting ready:
1. Dissolve the butter in the pan by putting it on low heat. Put the onion and garlic in a pan and let them fry for three minutes.

2. Mix carrot, celery, and chicken stock after some time have passed. Start the soup by boiling it.

3. Turn down the heat and cook for approximately half an hour at a low boil. After that, add the thyme, and keep the soup on low heat for another two minutes.

4. Pepper should be used to season them. Garnish them with some fresh parsley.

116. Wild Mushroom and Thyme Soup

What we need:

- 1 pound of sliced shiitake, oyster, or other varieties of mushrooms
- 5 cups veggie stock with no additional salt
- ½ cup of Greek yogurt that is plain and nonfat
- 1 medium-sized chopped sweet onion
- 4 tablespoons of vegetable oil
- Lime sap from one lemon
- 1 tablespoon worth of crushed garlic
- 2 teaspoons of freshly chopped thyme
- Black pepper that has been freshly grated, to taste

Cooking Method:

1. Once the pits have been removed from the dates, set them in a dish and wrap them with sweltering water.

2. Put a large pan that is filled with oil on the stove and bring it to cook over high heat. The onion and garlic should be stir so that they are transparent.

3. Put the mushrooms in a coating on a baking tray, and then set it in the microwave. Roast the mushrooms so that they get a color that is comparable to a light brown.

4. After adding the thyme, pour the broth and lime juice over the top of the mixture. Everything should be brought to cook, after which the heat should be reduced to a simmer, and it should be cooked for fifteen minutes until the vegetables are tender.

5. Take the soup off the heat, whisk in the yogurt, and then, just at the time of serve, flavor it with grated pepper.

117. Broccoli and Gold Potato Soup

What we need:

- Olive oil, one tablespoon
- ½ cup of diced onion
- 1 clove of garlic, finely crushed
- 4 cups of vegetable stew
- ¼ teaspoon of crushed red chili flakes
- 2 cups of chopped Yukon gold potatoes, peeled and weighed
- Florets of broccoli in the quantity of 2 cups
- ¼ teaspoons of thyme
- For garnish a quarter cup of chopped fresh chives

Cooking Method:

1. A big pot that has been completely filled with oil should be brought to cook on medium heat. Fry garlic and onion in olive oil so that the onion becomes translucent while being careful not to let the garlic get burned is the proper method.
2. After adding the potatoes, pour the vegetable stock over them. Keep it covered and let it boil.
3. Bring to a boil, immediately reduce the heat, and cook for a further fifteen minutes, or until the potato slices are as tender as you prefer.
4. After covering the pot and placing it over high heat, during the following five minutes, you should add the thyme as well as the red pepper flakes.
5. Put the broth in a food blender and blitz it until there are no lumps left. Pepper should be added to taste.
6. Place the soup in dishes and garnish with chives before serving.

118. Mushroom Barley Soup

What we need:

- Olive oil, two teaspoons
- 1 ounce of sliced carrots and 1 cup
- 1 measuring cup of diced onion
- Half a cup of diced celery
- 4 cups of button mushrooms that have been diced
- 1 cup of shiitake mushrooms that have been diced
- 2 cloves of garlic, chopped or crushed
- 1 ½ teaspoons of thyme, chopped
- Salt to taste
- 1 teaspoon of black pepper powder
- 2 glasses of milk derived from plants
- 1 ounce (or cup) of water
- 1/3 cup of barley that cooks quickly

Cooking Method:

1. Place your big saucepan with the oil in it over a medium heat. Within the space of three minutes, sauté all of the ingredients, except the barley, milk, and water.
2. Raise the flame to high and carry on cooking until the vast majority of the liquid has been absorbed.
3. After pouring the cream and water, add the barley to the mixture. Allow it to boil while stirring it often.
4. 4. Cook the barley for 15 minutes, reducing the heat to maintain a moderate simmer and stirring a few times during that time. After being ladled out, serve the soup immediately in the bowls it was prepared in.

119. Special Chicken Soup

What we need:

- 4 cups of vegetable broth
- A boneless, skinless chicken breast that is 4 ounces in weight
- ½ cup of cooked brown rice
- 1 jumbo-sized egg
- ⅛ cup of lemon juice that has been freshly squeezed
- ½ of lemon zest that has been grated
- ⅛ teaspoon of salt
- 1 eighth of a teaspoon of new black pepper

Cooking Method:

1. Place the broth in a cooker and then fetch it to steam over a medium-low flame using whatever heating method you like.
2. Roast the chicken for 15 to 20 minutes until it cooked well. Take the pan away from the heat as soon as possible.
3. Place the chicken in the bowl you have available and set it aside. After it has cooled, shred it with two forks.
4. Add the rice to the liquid, and then put the chicken back in the pot. Prepare over a heat source of medium intensity for about 15 minutes, or until soft. The heat should be set to medium-low.
5. Eggs, lime sap, and lemon zest should be mixed in a separate basin and whisked together.
6. To temper the sauce, whisk in a cup of the stock while adding a ladleful of the liquid to the combination of lemon and eggs.
7. After adding the egg mixture to the saucepan and whisking it for a full minute, set the pot over medium heat. After that, extract the pan from the flame of heat, and then season it to taste with pepper and salt. Dish up.

120. Lentil and Veggie Soup

What we need:
- 2 tablespoons of olive oil
- 1 diced onion, medium size
- 2 carrots cut into small pieces
- 1 cup of dry brown lentils, measured out.
- 1 can of low-sodium chopped tomatoes, 28 ounces in size
- Four cups' worth of water
- Lemon juice from one lemon
- Black pepper, grated to the desired degree

Cooking Method:
1. Fill a big cooker to the brim with oil and cook on medium to high heat. Carrots and onions should be cooked in a skillet until they are just starting to get soft.
2. Add the water, tomatoes, and lentils to the pot. Put it on to boil.
3. The cooking time for the lentils, which should be around 25 to 30 minutes, should be continued after the heat is turned down to cook. Take the casserole dish out of the microwave so that it is soft. Take the pot out of the microwave.
4. Take two cups of the mixture out of the pot, place them in a blender, and process them so that they are completely smooth.
5. After adding the lemon juice, season it with pepper to taste. Dish up.

121. White Bean Soup with Orange

What we need:
- Two tablespoons of olive oil
- 1 finely chopped, medium-sized onion
- 2 tablespoons of diced celery
- ½ teaspoon of salt
- ½ teaspoon of freshly grated black pepper
- Four cups' worth of water
- 2 cans of white beans, washed and drained, low-sodium, and each weighing 15 ounces
- 1 teaspoon of oregano, dry

- ½ of the zest from a medium orange 1 full cup of juice from a medium orange

Cooking Method:

1. Bring a big saucepan filled with oil up to temperature over medium-high heat.
2. Within four to six minutes, sauté the celery and onion until they have become softer. Add a little salt and pepper before serving.
3. Put the beans, water, and oregano into the pot. Put it on to boil. After bringing it to a gentle simmer, lower the heat and continue to simmer for fifteen minutes. Remove it from the heat source right away.
4. Orange juice and orange zest should be mixed together in a bowl. If you want, you may serve the soup with a little bit of extra olive oil poured on top.

122. Simple Tomato Basil Soup

What we need:

- Olive oil, one teaspoonful
- 1 ounce of finely chopped onion
- 4 cloves of garlic, finely chopped
- 7 cups of chopped fresh tomatoes, in total
- A half cup's worth of finely chopped fresh basil leaves
- Salt to taste
- 1 teaspoon of grated black pepper

Cooking Method:

1. Put your oil into a medium-sized saucepan, and then increase the temperature of the oil to medium-high.
2. While the olive oil is heating up in a skillet, add the garlic and onion to the pan.
3. After the onions have softened, add the tomatoes and continue to simmer as long as the tomatoes begin to break down.
4. Remove the basil; next, combine it with the pepper and salt that have been previously mixed in. Make a silky purée by using your blender to process the ingredients. Dish up.

DESSERT

123. Maple-Walnut Pots

What we need:

- ½ cup of unsweetened soy milk is required.
- ¼ teaspoons of pure vanilla essence
- 1½ teaspoons of plain gelatin
- ½ cup fat-free Greek yogurt with vanilla flavor
- ½ cup of fat-free or low-fat buttermilk
- ½ cup of honey
- A speck of salt from the ocean
- A garnish of 2 tablespoons of chopped walnuts

Cooking Method:

1. Put the soy milk, sugar, and vanilla essence into a small pot and bring it to a simmer. Stir the mixture often while cooking it for two minutes over medium heat until it reaches a temperature that is just slightly warmer than room temperature.

2. After adding the gelatin, heat the mixture for no more than three minutes, until it reaches a boiling point.

3. Remove the saucepan from the heat and set it somewhere out of the way to cool off.

4. After adding the other ingredients, with the exception of the walnuts, thoroughly combine them all with a whisk.

5. Transfer the mixture to two ramekins with a capacity of 6 ounces each, and put them in the freezer for a minimum of four hours so that they can become cold. Walnuts should be scattered on top of the dish before serving.

124. Blackberry-Thyme Granita

What we need:

- 4 and a half cups of fresh blackberries
- 1 lime's worth of juice
- ¼ cup of honey
- 1 tablespoon of freshly chopped thyme

Cooking Method:

1. Place all of the components in your blender and process until they form a homogeneous paste. Place it in the bowl after passing it through a sieve with a fine mesh.
2. Spread it onto a baking sheet with a rim that measures 9 by ½ inches. Freeze the mixture within four hours, scraping the container every half hour. Dish up.

125. Carrot Cookies with Chocolate Chip

What we need:

- 1 egg, big in size
- A third of a cup of almond meal
- A quarter cup of shredded carrots
- ⅛ cup of applesauce that has not been sweetened
- A quarter of a cup of dairy-free dark-colored chocolate chips
- 1 milliliter of unadulterated maple syrup
- ¼ teaspoon of the baking powder
- ½ teaspoon of cinnamon powder

Cooking Method:

1. Turn up the microwave. Prepare a parchment paper lining for your baking sheet.
2. In an enormous combining bowl, whisk the almond nutrition, baking powder, chocolate chips, carrots, applesauce, maple syrup, eggs, as well as grated cinnamon. Combine all of the ingredients by stirring each other until the mixture takes on the texture of thick dough.
3. Place tablespoon-sized rounds onto the baking sheet that has been prepared. Bake the bread for ten to fifteen minutes, so that it begins to become a light brown color. Dish up.

126. Banana-Oatmeal Cookies

What we need:

- ¼ cup olive oil, plus additional oil for greasing
- ¾ cup unadulterated honey
- 1 egg
- 2 very big, perfectly ripe bananas, mashed.
- 2 teaspoons of pure vanilla essence
- 1 cup of flour
- A pinch of kosher salt
- ½ teaspoons of baking soda
- 3.0 ounces of rolled oats

Cooking Method:

1. Bring the temperature of the microwave. Grease two baking tray with rims and set them aside with oil.
2. Take a big bowl, combine the egg, honey, and oil, and whisk them together. To that, add some bananas, followed by a thorough mixing of the ingredients.
3. Place all of the elements like salt, butter, and flour in a mixer and blend. Combine the banana mixture you already have with the flour mixture. Blend in the rolled oats.
4. Scoop out rounds the size of a tablespoon and place them on the baking sheets that have been prepared. Roast for 3 to 5 minutes, keeping a careful eye on it towards the end so that the cookies will not catch fire.
5. To serve.

127. Marinated Berries

What we need:

- 2 cups of fresh strawberries cubed
- 1/8 of a teaspoon of black pepper
- 1 cup of blueberries, if you want them
- A tablespoon's worth of balsamic vinegar
- 1 tablespoon of natural honey
- 3 tablespoons of mint, chopped

Cooking Method:

1. Combine the strawberries, blueberries (if desired), honey, and cinnamon in a large bowl.
2. Combine pepper, mint and vinegar in a big basin that is not reactive.
3. Give the flavors some time to come together for no less than 25 minutes and up to 2 hours.

128. Tofu Mocha Mousse

What we need:

- 4 ounces of dark chocolate with a percentage of 70%, cut very finely
- A quarter of a cup of unsweetened soy milk
- ½ teaspoon of espresso powder
- A half of a teaspoon of pure vanilla extract
- A speck of salt from the ocean
- 4 ounces of silken tofu, well drained

Cooking Method:

1. Put the chocolate in the bowl that's about the size of your palm and set it aside.
2. Put the soy milk, coffee powder, vanilla extract, and salt in a cooker. Place the cooker over medium flame. Get the mixture to cook.
3. Cook the mixer well, and then sprinkle it over the chocolate when it has cooked. After letting the mixture sit for ten minutes, whisk it until all of the ingredients are mutual.
4. Add it to the tofu in your blender and mix until smooth. Process it in a blender until it is completely smooth.
5. Divide the mixture into two dish, cover, and refrigerate the mixture for a minimum of two hours or until it solidifies. Dish up.

129. Dessert Made with Grilled Mango

What we need:

- 1 mango, peeled, seeded, and cut to your preference
- 1 lime, sliced into eight equal-sized wedges

Cooking Method:

1. The first step is to preheat both the microwave and the broiler, and then position the microwave's rack so that it is in the upper third of the microwave. Line the base of your broiler pan with aluminum foil.

2. Place the mango slices so that they are in a single layer in the pan that has been prepared—broil approximately eight to ten minutes, or until there are brown patches throughout.

3. Divide the mixture evenly between two dishes, then strain the lime wedges over the top and carry it out.

130. Date Brownies

What we need:

- 2 cups of dates with the pits removed
- 3 jumbo-sized eggs
- 1 standard cup of grated almonds
- ½ teaspoon of cocoa powder
- A quarter cup of avocado oil
- One teaspoon of baking soda
- A little bit of salt

Cooking Method:

1. Turn the microwave on to 350 degrees F and let it preheat. Spray some oil in your 8-inch baking dish, and then grease it.

2. Place your small pan of water on the stove and increase the temperature to a high setting. Removing the pan off the heat is an emergency.

3. Once the pits have been removed from the dates, set them in a bowl, cover them with water in a separate pot, and start to boil. Let them soak for 15 minutes. Empty out.

4. Put the dates and the two tablespoons of water into your food processor and pulse until combined to make a smoothie consistency.

5. Mix the eggs one by one, mixing in between each addition of an egg.

6. Stirring the dry ingredients together will combine all of the ingredients. Bake for thirty minutes, or until the dish can be pierced all the way through with a toothpick made of stainless steel and comes out clean.

7. Take the dish out of the microwave. After allowing it to cool, carve it into ¼ equal pieces. Dish up.

131. Yogurt and Berry Freezer Pops

What we need:

- 1 fluid ounce of either blueberries or blackberries that is fresh.
- ½ cup of Greek yogurt that is plain and nonfat.
- 2 tablespoons of natural honey
- 2 cups of low-fat milk

Cooking Method:

1. Put all of the ingredients into your blender and blitz them together until the combination is perfectly soft.
2. Remove the liquid to ice pop molds, and then store the molds in the freezer for at least six hours before serving.

132. Dark Chocolate and Cherry Trail Mix

What we need:

- 1 cup of almonds that have not been salted
- A third of a cup of dried cherries
- ½ cup chopped walnuts
- ½ cup of chickpeas that have been roasted with sugar and spice
- ¼ cup of broken pieces of dark chocolate

Cooking Method:

1. Place the almonds, cherries, walnuts, chickpeas, and chocolate chips in a container that can seal tightly.
2. Dish up.

133. Pumpkin Pie Fruit Leathers

What we need:

- 2 cups of pumpkin pie filling
- 1 cup of applesauce that has not been sweetened
- 1 tablespoon of pure maple syrup
- ¼ teaspoon of cinnamon powder
- ⅛ teaspoon of grated nutmeg

- ⅛ teaspoon of grated ginger
- A little bit of grated allspice (one pinch)

Cooking Method:

1. The first step is to preheat the microwave. In order to get your baking sheet ready, you need line it with parchment paper.
2. Take a medium dish, come together the pumpkin, applesauce, and cinnamon with a whisk till the maple syrup, cinnamon, nutmeg, ginger, and allspice are all incorporated and combined really smoothly.
3. Distribute the combination out on a baking sheet and roast it for 8 hours, or until it reaches the desired consistency and the whole thing is dry.
4. Take the leather out of the microwave, and then cut it up into ten separate pieces. Dish up.

134. Chilled Mango Yogurt Drink

What we need:

- 2 measuring cups of frozen mango pieces
- ½ cup of plain Greek yogurt with 2% fat
- ¼ cup of milk
- 2 teaspoons of unadulterated honey (optional)

Cooking Method:

1. Put both the yogurt and mango in a blender and mix them together. Slowly pour the milk into the cup over a period of time in order to get the texture of soft-serve ice cream.
2. Give it a taste, and if you like it, add more honey. Devour it without delay.

135. Wrapped with Almond Butter and Banana

What we need:

- 2 tablespoons of unsweetened almond butter
- 1 tortilla made with whole wheat
- 1 banana, peeled and sliced

Cooking Method:

1. Smear your tortilla with the almond butter.
2. Place the banana in the middle of the tortilla, and then encircle it with the tortilla.

3. If you want it chopped into three pieces, enjoy.

136. Cinnamon Pear Crisp

What we need:
- 3 medium pears, cored and sliced
- 2 tablespoons of pure maple sap, sliced in half
- ½ teaspoon of cinnamon powder
- A half cup of rolled oats, broken up
- ¼ cup of walnuts that have been chopped
- 1 ½ tablespoons of olive oil

Cooking Method:
1. Put the microwave on to preheat at 350°F.
2. Position the pears, three tablespoons of maple syrup, and cinnamon in the bowl you are using.
3. Evenly distribute the pears in the baking dish that is 8 inches in diameter.
4. Grind one-fourth of a cup of grains in your food processor, then transfer the grated oats to a smaller bowl.
5. Mix the rest of the oats and walnuts into the oat flour and mix well. Combine thoroughly.
6. Pure the remaining maple syrup and oil over the pancakes. Toss in order to coat. Crumble the mixture and swell over the apples in a layer.
7. The seventh step is to put it in the microwave and bake it for forty-five minutes, so that the top is golden brown. As soon as it has been removed from the microwave, it should be served.

137. Pumpkin Cakes Prepared in Ramekins

What we need:

- 4 teaspoons pure honey
- ¼ cup of pumpkin puree
- 1 teaspoon of almond milk, unsweetened
- ¼ cup of oat flour
- 2 tablespoons of olive oil
- 1 teaspoon of baking powder

Cooking Method:

1. Position a baking tray inside the preheated microwave and turn the temperature up to 350 degrees.
2. Combine the almond butter, pumpkin purée, and pumpkin pie spice in a small measuring dish. Honey, milk, olive oil, and the spice of pumpkin pie are the ingredients in this recipe.
3. Combine all of the dry components (salt, flour, and baking powder) in a basin designated for mixing.
4. When a toothpick inserted in the center of a muffin reveals no residue after being baked for 22 to 25 minutes in a microwave that has been preheated, the muffins are done. The mixture should be distributed in an even layer between two ramekins that are each 4 ounces in capacity.
5. Sprinkle an additional amount of the pumpkin pie spice over each serving.

SALADS

138. Quinoa Salad

What we need:

- 2 cups of quinoa that has been cooked
- ½ cups of grated Brussels sprouts, grated red cabbage, sliced carrots, yellow bell peppers that have been seeded and chopped, diced cucumber, and halved cherry tomatoes

Regarding the garnish:

- 4 tablespoons of lemon sap
- Kosher salt, one-fourth of a teaspoon, and powdered black pepper to taste
- 4 teaspoons of olive oil

Cooking Method:

1. To make the dressing, transfer all of its components into a separate, more compact dish. For the time being, set it aside.
2. Place one-fourth cup of each of the following vegetables on top of the quinoa in each of the four bowls: Brussels sprouts, cabbage, carrots, bell peppers, cucumbers, and tomatoes.
3. Add a few tablespoons of the dressing to each bowl, and then serve.

139. Orange Salad

What we need:

- 1 big bulb of fennel, peeled, trimmed, and cut very thinly
- 2 oranges, medium in size, peeled and sectioned
- 1 table spoon of olive oil
- 1 teaspoon of vinegar made from red wine
- Cranberries, dried, two tablespoons' worth
- To taste, season with grated black pepper and freshly ground salt.

Cooking Method:

1. Put the fennel and oranges in a big bowl and mix them together. Vinegar and oil should be drizzled over the meat before it is seasoned with salt and pepper.
2. After tossing the salad, place the cranberries on top of it. Serve.

140. Cucumber, Lemony Bulgur, and Lentil Salad

What we need:

- 2 cups of ready-to-eat bulgur
- 1 cup of washed and drained canned lentils with reduced sodium content
- 1 English cucumber
- ½ of a jalapeno pepper, diced
- ½ of a scallion, white and green parts chopped,
- ½ of a red bell pepper, thinly sliced, finely chopped
- 1 lemon, juice, and zest
- 1 tablespoon of natural honey
- 1 tablespoon of freshly chopped cilantro
- A garnish of 2 tablespoons of chopped roasted peanuts

Cooking Method:

1. Place the bulgur, lentils, cucumber, jalapeno, scallion, and bell pepper in a large bowl. Mix everything together by tossing it around.
2. Toss the mixture to coat it with honey, lemon juice, lemon zest, and cilantro, and then add the honey.
3. Place it in the refrigerator no more than half an hour after covering it in plastic wrap.
4. Top with chopped peanuts as a garnish.

141. Couscous Salad

What we need:

- 2 tablespoons of olive oil
- 2 teaspoons of salt
- 2 tablespoons of vinegar
- 2 teaspoons of black pepper
- 1 cup of couscous from Israel
- 1 ounce of water
- A cup and a half of cherry tomatoes, halved
- 1 chickpea can, drained and washed
- ¼ cups of fresh parsley, chopped and measured

Cooking Method:

1. In the smaller dish you have, create the vinaigrette by first whisking together 2 tablespoons of oil, the vinegar, a quarter teaspoon of pepper, and salt.
2. The remaining amount of oil must be moved to a big cooker and warmed up to a temperature that is somewhere between medium and high.
3. Continue to cook the couscous for a little more than two minutes or until it has a golden brown color. Pour the water, and then wait for it to come to a boil.
4. The remaining salt should be sprinkled in now. Adjust the temperature so that a simmer is maintained, and cook the couscous for around 10 minutes, or until it achieves the consistency you want. Take the dish away from the heat. After draining, lay it aside to chill off.
5. Take a big dish; combine the tomatoes, chickpeas, and vinaigrette all at once.
6. Stir the mixture one more time after adding the couscous. After allowing it to cool, mix in the parsley, and then serve.

142. Green Salad with Oranges and Avocados

What we need:

- ¼ cup of pistachios that have been shelled
- 1 big orange, cut in half and peeled
- 2 teaspoons of salt olive oil of an extra-virgin quality
- 2 tablespoons of unflavored yogurt
- 2 teaspoons of lemon juice that has been freshly squeezed
- 2 teaspoons of authentic maple syrup
- ¼ teaspoon of kosher salt
- Black pepper that has been freshly grated, to taste
- 2 heads of lettuce
- 1 avocado, peeled, seeded, and sliced up in small pieces

Cooking Method:

1. Preheat the microwave before using it.
2. Spread out your pistachios in a layer on a rimmed baking sheet and pop it in the microwave.
3. Roast the vegetables for a total of ½ minutes, turning them over twice. Wait for them to cool, and then coarsely cut them.

4. Pour the juice that was extracted from one half of the orange into a big basin.

5. Add the yogurt, lemon juice, olive oil, maple syrup, pepper, and salt, and combine the entire ingredients well.

6. Cut the flesh of the remaining orange half into small pieces after removing the peel.

7. In the dish containing the dressing, add the lettuce, orange slices, avocado, and pistachios, and mix everything together well.

143. Baked Beet Arugula Salad

What we need:

- 1 bunch of beets (three to four medium-sized)
- 1 bag of arugula, weighing eight ounces
- A quarter of a cup of balsamic vinaigrette
- A quarter of a cup of chopped almonds
- A quarter of a cup of goat cheese crumbles

Cooking Method:

1. Before using the microwave, make sure it has been preheated.

2. Bake the beets in the microwave for 25 to 35 minutes, after having been covered in aluminum foil and preheated, or until they can be readily pierced, whichever comes first. After baking, the beets should be easily piercable. Take it out of the microwave and set it aside. Let it cool until it becomes manageable.

3. Remove the skins from the beets by sliding them off with your hands and discarding them. Next, cut the beets into wedges.

4. Put the beets and arugula in a large basin and mix them together with a fork. After giving the vinaigrette over the beets, you should make sure to give them a little spin before serving.

5. After you have sprinkled the cheese and almonds on the salad, it is ready to be served.

144. Chickpea and Tomato Salad

What we need:

- One-half can (7 ounces) of chickpeas with no additional salt, which have been washed and drained
- 1 tomato, diced, plum type
- ½ cup of fresh cilantro that has been chopped
- ⅛ cup of red onion that has been coarsely chopped
- ½ of a lemon's worth of zest and juice
- 1 teaspoon of grated cumin
- ½ teaspoon of olive oil, extra-virgin
- 1 teaspoon of honey
- Black pepper that has been freshly grated, to taste

Cooking Method:

1. Place all of the ingredients in the bowl that you will be using. Serve it.

145. Quinoa and Spinach Salad

What we need:

- 1 ounce of water
- ¼ cup quinoa, washed and drained, which has not been cooked.
- 1 cup of chopped spinach, very coarsely
- ½ measuring spoon of sweet snap peas
- ¼ of a cup of tomato chunks
- ¼ cup of cucumbers cut into dice
- A quarter of a cup of sliced almonds

Regarding the garnish:

- ½ milliliter of lemon juice that has been freshly squeezed
- 1 tablespoon of olive oil
- ⅛ teaspoon of freshly roasted black pepper ⅛ teaspoon of salt

Cooking Method:

1. Bring a medium-sized saucepan's worth of water to a boil. After adding the quinoa, continue to simmer for another 10 minutes, so that the quinoa is soft. Drain it, and then let it cool.

2. In a large bowl, combine the quinoa that has been cooked with the other ingredients for the salad.

3. In the smaller dish, mix together the elements for the dressing. Put it over the top portion of your salad, give it a good spin, and then serve it.

146. Tuna, Cashew, and Couscous Salad

What we need:
- A half cup of uncooked whole-wheat couscous and a quarter teaspoon of salt
- 1 can of tuna sourced responsibly, packaged in oil, drained, and mashed
- 1 cup diced yellow and red bell peppers
- 1 package of broccoli slaw, weighing in at ½ ounces
- Three scallions were cut very finely.
- Three tablespoons of vinegar
- 2 tablespoons of extra-virgin olive oil
- 1 teaspoon of oregano, dry
- 1 teaspoon of thyme, dried
- ½ teaspoon of black pepper that has been freshly grated
- ½ cups of chopped, roasted cashews that are unsalted

Cooking Method:
1. Prepare the couscous with the salt in accordance with the instructions on the box. Place the cooled couscous in the big bowl and set it aside to cool completely.

2. Add any leftover components to the mixture.

3. Serve, please.

147. Avocado Salad with Roasted Carrots

What we need:

- 1 cup of tiny carrots cut in half along their length
- Salt
- 1 tablespoon of vegetable oil
- ⅛ teaspoon of freshly grated black pepper
- ½ of a can of chickpeas (15 ounces), drained and rinsed
- 2 tablespoons of walnuts that have been roughly chopped
- 4 cups of kale, cut roughly and stemmed, that has been massaged until it is pliable
- 2 teaspoons of lemon juice that has been freshly squeezed
- 1 huge, perfectly ripe avocado, peeled, seeded, and chopped into cubes

Cooking Method:

1. Bring the temperature inside the microwave for the preheating process.
2. Spread out a layer of carrots on a sheet of parchment paper. Shake over them with oil, and then flavor with pepper and salt to taste. Then cook at 400 degrees for twenty minutes.
3. After adding the chickpeas and walnuts, give everything a thorough shake, and then roast it once more during the next five to ten minutes.
4. Place the greens, lemon sap, and avocado in a large mixing basin and stir to blend.
5. Add half of the carrot combination and mix it well before adding the other half. Spread the leftover carrot combination and avocado on top of the salad. Dish up.

A 30 DAYS MEAL PLAN

DAY	Breakfast	Lunch	Dinner
1	Chia Seed Pudding	Keto Beef and Broccoli Stir-Fry	Rice and Beef Soup
2	Avocado and Bacon Egg Cups	Spaghetti Squash-Sausage Casserole	Cheesy Tuna Casserole
3	Omelet	Easy Cheesy Bacon Quiche	Slow-Cooker Pizza
4	Chicken with Green Beans	Shrimp Stir-Fry	Holiday Lamb with Asparagus
5	Broccoli and Pasta	Chicken Soup with Noodle	Zoodles with meatballs in an Italian sauce
6	Waffle Sandwich	Chicken and Vegetable Soup	Curry with Spinach and Lamb
7	Berry Chia Pudding	Buffalo Cauliflower Bites	Curried cauliflower soup
8	Butter Mocha Latte	Buffalo Cauliflower Bites	Walleye Simmered in Basil Cream
9	Spinach and Feta Breakfast Wrap	Grilled Chicken Caesar Salad	Italian Loaf of Meat
10	Turkey Casserole	Chicken Balls	Walleye Simmered in Basil Cream
11	Blueberry-Banana Smoothies	Shrimp Paella	Italian Style Roast in a Pot
12	Lime Chicken	Meatloaf	Cilantro-lime Flounder
13	Avocado and Bacon Egg Cups	Spaghetti Squash-Sausage Casserole	Chili Verde
14	Bagel Sandwich with Goat Cheese	Chicken and Vegetable Soup	Curried cauliflower soup
15	Pizza Casserole	Easy Cheesy Bacon Quiche	Pulled Pork with Apricots

16	Greek Yogurt Parfait	Chicken Soup with Noodle	Buffalo Chicken Tacos
17	Almond-Apricot Granola	Zoodles Alfredo with Grilled Chicken	Italian Style Roast in a Pot
18	Smoked Salmon and Cream Cheese Roll-Ups	Shrimp Stir-Fry	French Style Potato Fries
19	Avocado and Bacon Egg Cups	Cashew Chicken	Cauliflower Hash Browns
20	Broccoli and Pasta	Grilled Chicken Caesar Salad	Slow-Cooker Pizza
21	Bagel Sandwich with Goat Cheese	Chicken Vegetable soup	Curry with Spinach and Lamb
22	Blueberry-Banana Smoothies	Cabbage and Beef Stir-Fry	Cilantro-lime Flounder
23	Butter Mocha Latte	Meatloaf	Zoodles with meatballs in an Italian sauce
24	Turkey Casserole	Easy Cheesy Bacon Quiche	Tuna with Zoodles Casserole
25	Greek Yogurt Parfait	Eggplant Lasagna	Italian Loaf of Meat
26	Almond-Apricot Granola	Shrimp Paella	French Style Potato Fries
27	Chicken with Green Beans	Spaghetti Squash-Sausage Casserole	Pulled Pork with Apricots
28	Spinach and Feta Breakfast Wrap	Zoodles Alfredo with Grilled Chicken	Holiday Lamb with Asparagus
29	Lime Chicken	Cabbage and Beef Stir-Fry	Buffalo Chicken Tacos
30	Waffle Sandwich	Easy Cheesy Bacon Quiche	Chili Verde

CONCLUSION

As we bring this culinary symphony to a close, "Dr. Nowzaradan's Cookbook" stands as a testament to the harmonious intersection of health and flavor. This collection of recipes is more than a mere guided; it's a crescendo of nutritional wisdom and culinary artistry orchestrated by the renowned Dr. Younan Nowzaradan.

In these pages, you've explored a medley of vibrant, elements that are low in carbohydrates and not only will please your taste senses but will also nourish your body. This cookbook isn't just about adhering to a ketogenic lifestyle; it's a celebration of the diverse and delicious ways in which you can achieve your health goals. Dr. Nowzaradan's meticulous approach to keto cuisine ensures that each dish is not only a delight to the senses but a step toward transformative well-being.

As you bid adieu to this culinary journey, take with you the understanding that a healthy lifestyle is not synonymous with sacrifice. "Keto Symphony" has been a guide to redefining your relationship with food, turning your kitchen into a stage for wellness. The grand finale is not just the last page of a cookbook; it's the beginning of a sustained, joyful approach to eating, where each meal is an opportunity to nourish your body and delight your palate.

May the echoes of this culinary symphony resonate in your daily choices, invigorating you to design, experiment, and take pleasure in the plethora of tastes that are beneficial to your quest toward better health? You may be a seasoned keto aficionado or just starting out or a newcomer to the low-carb lifestyle, let the notes of wellness linger in your kitchen, reminding you that every meal is a chance to compose a healthier, happier you. Thank you for joining us on this flavorful voyage. May your health continue to be a symphony of well-chosen ingredients, vibrant tastes, and lasting vitality?

Made in the USA
Coppell, TX
15 January 2025